Macmillan/McGraw-

WAVE ENERGY

AUTHORS

Mary Atwater
The University of Georgia

Prentice Baptiste
University of Houston

Lucy Daniel
Rutherford County Schools

Jay Hackett
University of Northern Colorado

Richard Moyer
University of Michigan, Dearborn

Carol Takemoto
Los Angeles Unified School District

Nancy Wilson
Sacramento Unified School District

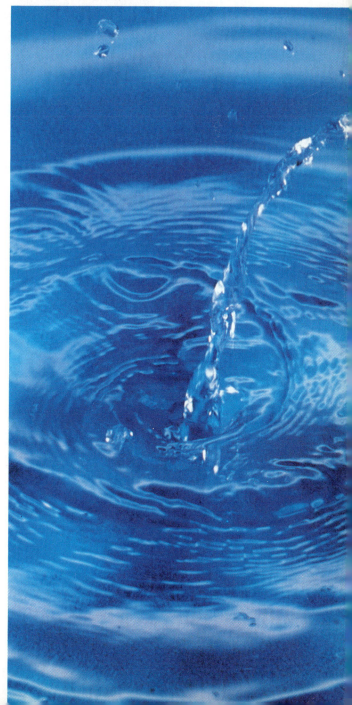

Water waves in motion

**Macmillan/McGraw-Hill
School Publishing Company
New York   Columbus**

MACMILLAN / McGRAW-HILL

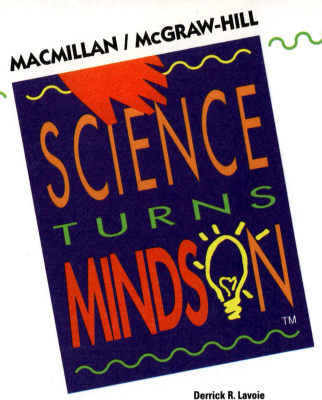

CONSULTANTS

Assessment:
Mary Hamm
Associate Professor
Department of Elementary Education
San Francisco State University
San Francisco, CA

Cognitive Development:
Pat Guild, Ed.D.
Director, Graduate Programs in Education and Learning Styles Consultant
Antioch University
Seattle, WA

Kathi Hand, M.A.Ed.
Middle School Teacher and Learning Styles Consultant
Assumption School
Seattle, WA

Derrick R. Lavoie
Assistant Professor of Science Education
Montana State University
Bozeman, MT

Earth Science:
David G. Futch
Associate Professor of Biology
San Diego State University
San Diego, CA

Dr. Shadia Rifai Habbal
Harvard-Smithsonian Center for Astrophysics
Cambridge, MA

Tom Murphree, Ph.D.
Global Systems Studies
Monterey, CA

Suzanne O'Connell
Assistant Professor
Wesleyan University
Middletown, CT

Sidney E. White
Professor of Geology
The Ohio State University
Columbus, OH

Environmental Education:
Cheryl Charles, Ph.D.
Executive Director
Project Wild
Boulder, CO

Gifted:
Dr. James A. Curry
Associate Professor, Graduate Faculty
College of Education, University of Southern Maine
Gorham, ME

Global Education:
M. Eugene Gilliom
Professor of Social Studies and Global Education
The Ohio State University
Columbus, OH

Life Science:
Wyatt W. Anderson
Professor of Genetics
University of Georgia
Athens, GA

Orin G. Gelderloos
Professor of Biology and Professor of Environmental Studies
University of Michigan—Dearborn
Dearborn, MI

Donald C. Lisowy
Education Specialist
New York, NY

Dr. E.K. Merrill
Assistant Professor
University of Wisconsin Center—Rock County
Madison, WI

Literature:
Dr. Donna E. Norton
Texas A&M University
College Station, TX

Copyright © 1995 Macmillan/McGraw-Hill School Publishing Company

All rights reserved. No part of this book may be reproduced or transmitted in any form or by any means, electronic or mechanical, including photocopying, recording, or by any information storage and retrieval system, without permission in writing from the publisher.

**Macmillan/McGraw-Hill School Division
10 Union Square East
New York, New York 10003
Printed in the United States of America**

ISBN 0-02-276133-0 / 7

4 5 6 7 8 9 RRW 99 98 97 96

Mathematics:
Dr. Richard Lodholz
Parkway School District
St. Louis, MO

Middle School Specialist:
Daniel Rodriguez
Principal
Pomona, CA

Misconceptions:
Dr. Charles W. Anderson
Michigan State University
East Lansing, MI

Dr. Edward L. Smith
Michigan State University
East Lansing, MI

Multicultural:
Bernard L. Charles
Senior Vice President
Quality Education for Minorities Network
Washington, DC

Paul B. Janeczko
Poet
Hebron, MA

James R. Murphy
Math Teacher
La Guardia High School
New York, NY

Clifford E. Trafzer
Professor and Chair, Ethnic Studies
University of California, Riverside
Riverside, CA

Physical Science:
Gretchen M. Gillis
Geologist
Maxus Exploration Company
Dallas, TX

Henry C. McBay
Professor of Chemistry
Morehouse College and Clark Atlanta University
Atlanta, GA

Wendell H. Potter
Associate Professor of Physics
Department of Physics
University of California, Davis
Davis, CA

Claudia K. Viehland
Educational Consultant, Chemist
Sigma Chemical Company
St. Louis, MO

Reading:
Charles Temple, Ph.D.
Associate Professor of Education
Hobart and William Smith Colleges
Geneva, NY

Safety:
Janice Sutkus
Program Manager: Education
National Safety Council
Chicago, IL

Science Technology and Society (STS):
William C. Kyle, Jr.
Director, School Mathematics and Science Center
Purdue University
West Lafayette, IN

Social Studies:
Jean Craven
District Coordinator of Curriculum Development
Albuquerque Public Schools
Albuquerque, NM

Students Acquiring English:
Mario Ruiz
Pomona, CA

STUDENT ACTIVITY TESTERS

Alveria Henderson
Kate McGlumphy
Katherine Petzinger
John Wirtz
Sarah Wittenbrink
Andrew Duffy
Chris Higgins
Sean Pruitt
Joanna Huber
John Petzinger

FIELD TEST TEACHERS

Kathy Bowles
Landmark Middle School
Jacksonville, FL

Myra Dietz
#46 School
Rochester, NY

John Gridley
H.L. Harshman Junior High School #101
Indianapolis, IN

Annette Porter
Schenk Middle School
Madison, WI

Connie Boone
Fletcher Middle School
Jacksonville, FL

Theresa Smith
Bates Middle School
Annapolis, MD

Debbie Stamler
Sennett Middle School
Madison, WI

Margaret Tierney
Sennett Middle School
Madison, WI

Mel Pfeiffer
I.P.S. #94
Indianapolis, IN

CONTRIBUTING WRITER

Katherine Kenah

Waves can reshape the shoreline.

Wave Energy

Lessons **Themes**

Unit Introduction **Wave Energy** .... Energy **6**
Can you imagine Earth without a bird's song or the warmth of the sun?
Find out how these waves affect Earth.

1 **What Are Properties of Waves?** .... Energy **12**
What do the movements of a stretched rubber band have in common
with waves?

2 **Quiet Out There!** .... Energy **26**
Why are some sounds pleasing and others painful?

3 **What Is That Strange Sound?** .... Energy **38**
Musicians and scientists each measure sound—but are they measuring
the same thing?

4 **What Is Light and What Are Its Properties?** .... Energy **52**
Light follows the rules—learn the rules and their uses.

5 **Refraction—What Happens When Light Is Bent?** .... Energy **70**
What do mirages and eyeglasses have in common? Read this lesson
to understand refraction.

6 **How Does a Prism Separate White Light Into Colors?** ...... Energy **82**
Learn the secrets scientists know about color—it's not what you think
it might be. Read this lesson to learn the surprising facts about colors.

Unit Wrap Up **Waves in Your World** .... Energy **96**
Put your knowledge of waves to work in a dangerous situation.

EXPLORE
Determining Wave Properties 14
How Are Sounds Produced? 28
Making Sounds With Bottles 40
Reflection of Light 56
How Can You Bend Light? 72
Spinning Color 86

TRY THIS
Wave Motion 9
Waves Transfer Energy 17
Tank Waves 19
Elastic Wave Machine 21
Wave Interference 22
Producing Sound 31
What Wave Is This? 32
Frequency and Pitch 43
Making Louder Sounds 45
What Can You See in the Dark? ... 53
Rope Waves 58
Comparing Light Reflection 63
Traveling Light Rays 64
What Happened to the Light? 65
Make a Periscope 66
Is This Real? 71
Observing Lenses 76
Lenses at Work 78
Color Images 85
White Light and Colors: What
  Makes Up White Light? 88
Is This a Color Test? 91
Pouring Light 92
How Will You Communicate
  With the World? 96

Features

Links

Literature **L**ink
Science in Literature 10
Nutty Knows All 59
Optics: Light for a New Age 94

Language **A**rts **L**ink
Read With Sound Effects 51
Words and Lenses 79

Math **L**ink
Wave Speed 20
Timing Sound 34

CAREERS
Fishing With Sonar 36
Sound Effects Artist 50

SCIENCE TECHNOLOGY AND Society

Focus on Technology
Smart Building 23

Focus on Environment
Noise Pollution 34

Focus on Environment
Hold the Noise! 48

Focus on Technology
Let There Be Sound! 49

Focus on Technology
The Hubble Telescope 68

Departments
Glossary 98
Index 100
Credits 102

Theme T ENERGY

Wave Energy

Imagine the many ways waves are transmitting energy within this large city.

Minds On! What is a wave? Can you think of any examples of waves? What do you think it would be like on Earth if waves didn't exist? In what ways would Earth be different? Could you live on, or visit, Planet Earth?

Imagine waking one morning in a world of total darkness. You're breathing heavily inside a spacesuit because oxygen and heat are missing from the atmosphere. The alarm clock doesn't glow or ring beside your bed. The radio is silent. No matter which dial you turn, the television channels remain blank. No voices call you to hurry and get dressed. How can you tell if it's time to get up for school? The silence is as total as the darkness. You feel your way to the kitchen, but the cupboards are empty. Every bit of food has vanished. In fact, in a world without waves, you might as well go back to bed. School will be canceled for the day...along with most life on the planet.

When many people think of waves, they think of ocean waves. However, islands aren't the only things surrounded by waves. You are surrounded and bombarded by them daily.

A wave is a disturbance that transfers energy. Energy is the ability to do work. The energy transmitted by ocean waves enables them to erode a sand castle on the beach, reshape a shoreline, or destroy a fishing village. The energy transmitted by sound waves brings music to our ears by causing our eardrums to move back and forth. It carries the voices of friends, the songs of birds, and the blaring warnings of fire alarms. It allows us to know when it's time to change classes. Light waves enable us to see and are indirectly responsible for our respiration and nutrition. They transmit the energy to make a potato grow, melt the snow, warm Earth, and make a flower blossom.

Large amounts of energy are being transferred by these water waves.

The sun radiates light energy in the form of waves.

Like students in your school, or shoes in a shopping mall, waves come in all different kinds and sizes. But despite their differences, waves share some common characteristics.

A wave transfers energy, but not matter, along its path. What is the difference, then, between energy and matter? Matter is anything that takes up space and has mass. Matter makes up everything in the universe that can be touched or shaped, grown or built. Energy is the ability to do work, and it moves in waves through matter or space. Energy carried by waves is transferred to whatever stops a wave.

Water waves and sound waves are caused when something disturbs a medium. A medium is simply the substance or matter that a wave moves through. Water is the medium of an ocean wave. Sound waves travel through solids, liquids, and gases. Your voice travels through the air as well as through solids and liquids. Beluga whales click and squeak to communicate underwater. You can feel the beat of music through a wall. Earth is the medium of seismic (earthquake) waves.

Some waves are different, however. They can travel and transmit energy in the absence of any medium. These waves are called electromagnetic (i lek′trō- mag net′ik) waves. Light waves, radio and television signals, microwaves, and X rays are all examples of electromagnetic waves. They can transmit energy through a vacuum, including outer space.

Solar flares represent the vast amount of energy given off by the sun.

Sound waves can be transmitted underwater.

The energy transmitted by ocean waves gives them the power to reshape a shoreline.

TRY THIS Activity!

Wave Motion

Using your previous knowledge of waves, you can predict and observe wave motion.

What You Need

cork, bowl, water
Activity Log page 1

Predict what will happen if you drop a cork into a bowl of water. Now drop the cork into a bowl of water and observe what happens. What is the medium of the wave? How is it moving? What is the direction of the wave energy being transmitted? Record your observations in your *Activity Log*.

Literature  Link

Science in Literature

The fascination of science never ends. Coupled with literature, it becomes more exciting, challenging each of us to explore our world in a way that has entertained humankind for centuries—exploration through the eyes of a book. Reading the following books can take you on a voyage into the world of waves, giving you firsthand information on the many ways waves transfer energy throughout the universe.

Optics: Light for a New Age by Jeff Hecht.
New York: Charles Scribner's Sons, 1987.

Ranging from the functioning of the human eye to the use of laser treatment to preserve eyesight, this book traces the development of optics. The book describes how optical devices are making light for a new age, a time of exciting advances and highly modern technology. You will discover the wonders of light and optics and many examples that relate to your everyday world.

Nutty Knows All by Dean Hughes.
New York: Atheneum, 1988.

Nutty Nutsell is known around school for his famous "nutty" science fair projects. This year Nutty is determined to show the boys around school that he isn't as stupid as they think. In this book, Nutty seeks the help of his genius buddy, William Bilks, to devise a project in which Nutty's brain waves communicate with the subatomic photons in light waves. The project ends up being slightly more than Nutty hoped for. He begins to feel and act strangely and his head glows in the dark. In the end, Nutty's experience with the photons helps the boys discover aspects of the "real" world that they had not noticed before.

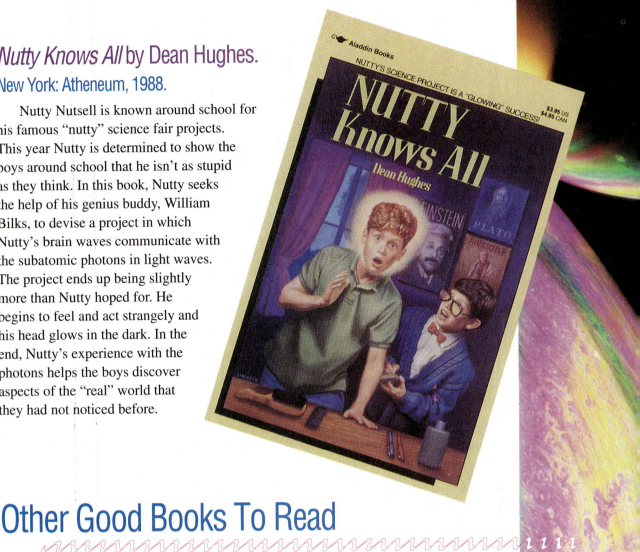

Other Good Books To Read

Lights, Lenses, and Lasers by M. Berger.
New York: G. P. Putnam's Sons, 1987.

Light is explained in an illustrated, easy-to-understand format that explores what light is and how we measure, record, perceive, and use it.

The Electromagnetic Spectrum by Franklyn M. Branley.
New York: Thomas Y. Crowell, 1979.

This book clearly introduces the techniques of investigating the universe—from the microworld of atoms to the macroworld of galaxies.

Radio: From Marconi to the Space Age by Alden R. Carter.
New York: Franklin Watts, 1987.

This book gives a history of radio wave transmission from the early 1900s to today, as well as projections toward the year 2000.

Exploring With Lasers by Brent Filson.
New York: Julian Messner, 1984.

This book relates energy to the real world by presenting information on how lasers are made, how they work, and how they are used.

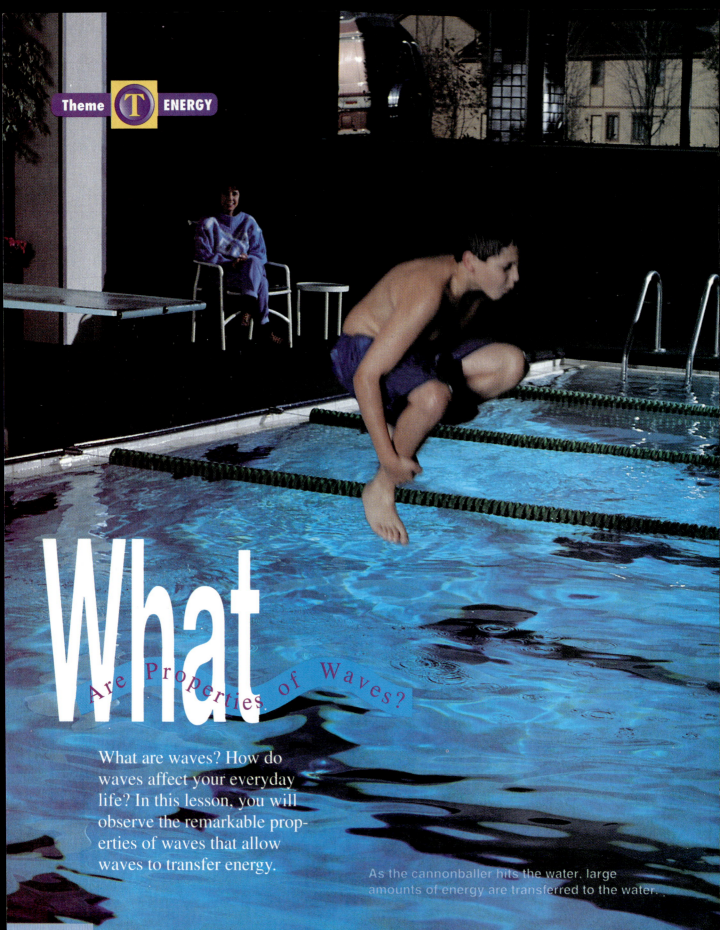

Theme T ENERGY

What Are Properties of Waves?

What are waves? How do waves affect your everyday life? In this lesson, you will observe the remarkable properties of waves that allow waves to transfer energy.

As the cannonballer hits the water, large amounts of energy are transferred to the water.

Have you ever been floating on an inner tube, eyes closed, basking in the sun, when someone on the diving board yells "Cannonball!" and plunges into the pool? Your eyes pop open. You see waves moving toward you across the surface of the water, and you grab the sides of the inner tube. But something strange happens. You probably don't tip over. You are not swept to the side of the pool. Instead the waves slide past you, bobbing you up and down and back and forth, as they appear to move on across the water. You and your inner tube are still in about the same place in the pool.

What do you think happened? Why didn't the waves push you to the side of the pool? Recall that a wave is a disturbance that transmits energy and not matter. Changes occur in matter when energy is transferred to it. Because energy can do work, it can move matter.

Both you and your inner tube are matter. So how did you change? You pretty much stayed in the same place in the pool instead of moving in the direction of the wave energy. The energy of the wave, however, caused you to move up and down in the pool. Wave energy was transferred to your up-and-down motion. Water is matter, too. How do you think the water was moved by the wave? The wave energy worked on the water by moving it repeatedly up and down as this energy passed along the surface. From these observations, what can you conclude about how energy is transferred?

Minds On!

Think about floating in a pool on an inner tube. In your *Activity Log* on page 2, make a stick-figure side-view sketch of yourself on the tube, bobbing up and down in the water. Draw a wave that has passed under you and is moving away from you across the surface of the pool. Now, draw a straight line in the direction that both you and the inner tube are moving. Then draw a straight line in the direction the wave is moving. Extend the lines so they meet, or intersect. How would you describe the angle formed by the intersection of these two lines? How did the wave move you up and down at a right angle (90°) to its own motion? ●

Think again about the waves created in the pool when the cannonballer hit the water. How would these waves compare to those that would be created by someone gracefully diving into the water headfirst? The diver would also create water waves. Even though both of these sets of waves were created in the same medium— the water in the pool — they varied in size and shape. How do you think waves can change their shape and size as they transmit energy from one place to another? The source of a wave is the disturbance that sets it in motion or, in these examples, persons jumping into or diving into water. Wind is most frequently the source of water waves. You will act as the source of waves in the next activity as you investigate the properties of waves. You will also find out how the properties of waves, such as size and shape, can vary.

Water transfers energy from one place to another by wave movement.

EXPLORE Activity!

Determining Wave Properties

In what ways can you observe some properties of waves?

What You Need

spring toy
meter tape
safety goggles
Activity Log pages 3–4

What To Do

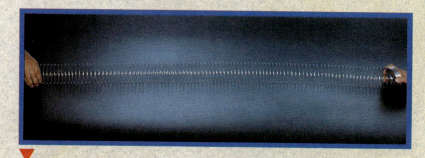

 Safety! Wear your goggles throughout this activity.

1 Have a partner hold one end of the spring toy without moving. Take hold of the other end and stretch the spring to a length of 3 m along a smooth floor.

2 Give one quick side-to-side motion to your end of the spring. Observe the spring.

3 Make a steady side-to-side motion so that one wave, one "hill" and one "valley," is formed with the entire spring.

4 Now, make the spring move twice as fast. Observe the number of waves and the length of each wave.

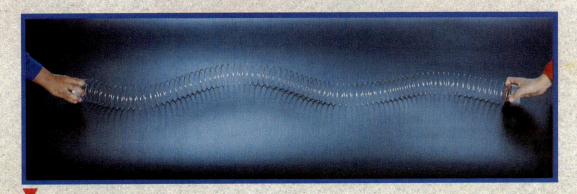

5 Repeat step 4 trying to move the spring twice as fast again. Note the number of waves and the lengths of the waves.

What Happened?

1. What happened in step 2 when the wave reached your partner? Turn to your **Activity Log** and enter your answers. How did the number of waves in step 4 compare with the number of waves in step 3?
2. How did the lengths of the waves in step 4 and step 3 compare?
3. How did the number of waves in step 5 compare with the number of waves in step 4? How did the lengths of the waves in step 5 and step 4 compare?

What Now?

1. Based on what you observed in step 2, how does a wave behave when it reaches a barrier?
2. If you increase the number of waves you make in a given time, how does the length of the sets of waves compare?

EXPLORE

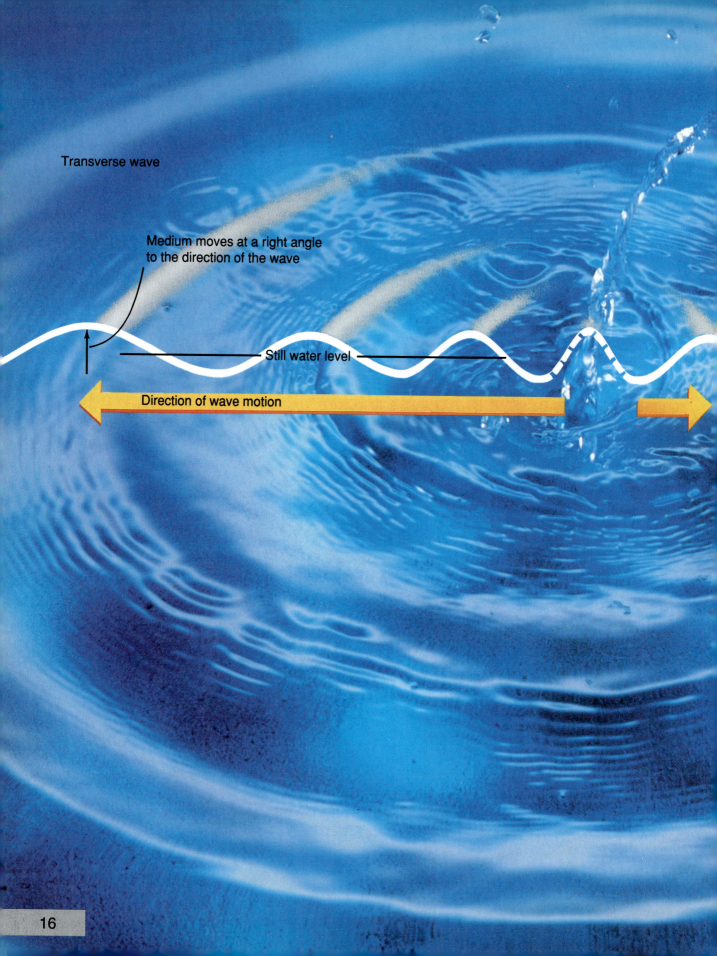

Wave Properties

Water transmits energy in the form of waves. As you discovered in the example of the inner tube floating in water, matter is not transmitted by waves. A water wave can be modeled by a transverse (trans vûrs′) wave. In a **transverse wave,** the matter in the medium moves at right angles to the direction the wave travels. Water was the medium of the waves in the pool. You and the inner tube were disturbed by the water because you were resting on the water. As a result, you were displaced in an up-and-down direction, while the waves moved energy across the surface of the pool. Observe how matter and energy move in the waves you create in the activity to the right.

When you walk to school or to the store, you may cross a number of blocks between your house and your destination. If the blocks are the same size, you encounter intersections at regular intervals. You walk a block and come to an intersection. You walk the same distance again and come to another intersection, over and over. There is a regular pattern to the route you are taking.

Similarly, waves can have regular patterns. Imagine riding a roller coaster shaped like the waves you just made in the pan. The car you are riding in clanks to the very top of the first hill, then races down. Before you can catch your breath and stop screaming, you are racing up the next hill. Again and again, up and down, your car moves over a regular pattern of rising and falling tracks. If you could imagine the feeling of this ride without the forward motion, you would feel as if you were bobbing up and down on a water wave.

TRY THIS Activity!

Waves Transfer Energy

How can you demonstrate the transfer of energy by waves?

What You Need
small cork
rectangular pan
water
Activity Log page 5

1. Put a small cork into a small rectangular pan of water.
2. To produce waves, pick up one end of the pan an inch or so and then lower it quickly back to the table. It will slosh a bit at first. Repeat this motion several times until a pattern is established.

3. Observe the cork.
4. Observe the motion of the water. What is moving across the pan? How can you be sure the waves are transmitting energy and not matter as they move?
5. Record all observations in your *Activity Log*.

The top of each hill, like the top of a wave, is called the **crest** (krest). The **trough** (trôf) of a wave is its lowest part and is similar to the valley between two hills. If you stopped the roller coaster on one hill and measured the distance to the exact same point on the next hill, the distance measured would be the length of one wave, or **wavelength.** Similarly, the wavelength of a water wave is the distance from crest to crest, or trough to trough, of two neighboring waves.

Another property of a wave is its frequency (frē′kwən sē). **Frequency** is simply the number of times something occurs in a given time period. To understand frequency, think about a newspaper route. The people on your route only subscribe to the Sunday paper. Therefore, you deliver papers once every seven days. The frequency of your newspaper deliveries is one time per week. Now suppose that you talk all of the people on your route into subscribing to the daily paper as well. The frequency of your deliveries increases to seven times per week.

Now, let's look back at the spring toy activity you did. What happened as you moved your wrist faster and faster? What can you say about the frequency of those waves? What happened to the size of the waves?

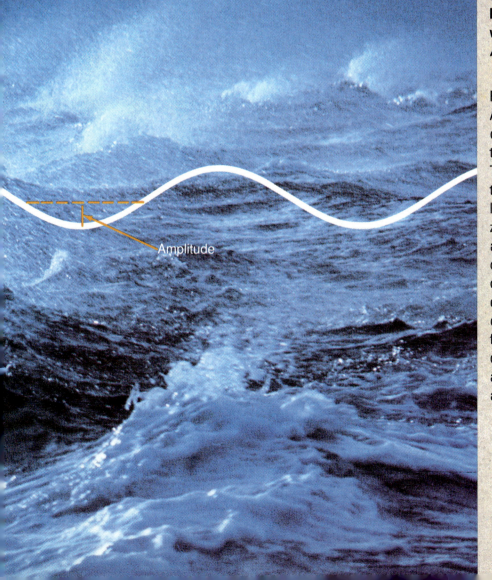

The amount of energy you used when you shook your wrist back and forth also affected the spring toy waves you made by changing their height, or amplitude (am′ pli tüd′). **Amplitude** is one-half the height of the wave from the crest to the trough. If you had measured the height of the spring toy during the activity, you would have found the amplitude of a transverse wave. The amplitude of a wave is related to the amount of energy put into the wave. In the activity, if you put a lot of energy into the spring toy by shaking it hard, you created waves with large amplitudes. If you put less energy into the spring toy, the waves had a smaller amplitude. As you can see, the amplitude of a wave is not determined by the wave's length or frequency. Do the activity on this page to find out what happens to water waves when you put more energy into them.

Amplitude

TRY THIS Activity!

Tank Waves

What can you observe about the characteristics of waves in a wave tank? Oceanographers frequently study the motions of waves with wave tanks. You can easily create your own wave tank.

What You Need

**tall, narrow glass jar with lid
cold water
blue food coloring
vegetable oil**
Activity Log **page 6**

Find a tall, narrow glass jar. Fill it one-third full of cold water. Add a few drops of blue food coloring, close the lid, and swirl the jar to mix the color evenly. Then, carefully fill the jar to the top with vegetable oil. Screw the lid on tightly. Hold the jar horizontally and move it gently back and forth to simulate the motion of water waves. Next, use more of a rocking motion to put more energy into the waves without changing their wavelengths and frequencies. In your **Activity Log,** describe what happens to the amplitude of the waves as you apply more energy to them.

Factors That Affect Wave Motion

So far in this lesson, we have seen characteristics of waves using water as the medium in which the waves transfer energy. Water, however, is not the only medium in which waves can transfer energy. Waves can conduct energy through solids, liquids, and gases. Some waves can even transfer energy through a vacuum, which is empty space! You will read about all of these waves in the lessons that follow.

All of the waves that you study in this unit have common characteristics that you have already identified in water waves. These characteristics are wavelength, frequency, and amplitude. You can determine the speed of three sets of water waves in the Math Link.

Math  Link

Wave Speed

The speed of a wave can be found by multiplying its frequency times its wavelength. Imagine you are sitting on the edge of a dock watching waves go by. Ten wave crests are passing every minute. The wavelength of these waves is three meters. Suddenly the sky grows cloudy. The breeze picks up. Now 20 wave crests are passing you each minute. If the wavelength remains the same, what has happened to the wave speed? What if the frequency increased to 30 wave crests per minute, but the wavelength shrank by one-third? How would the wave speed change?

Look at the diagram on this page. Notice that waves can have the same wavelengths and different frequencies. If you multiply the frequency of a wave by its wavelength, you determine the speed of the wave. What's the speed of each of the waves in the diagram? What happens to the speed if the frequency doubles and the wavelength remains the same? What happens to the frequency if the wavelength decreases and the speed remains the same? Another factor that affects the speed of a wave is the density of the material through which it is moving. For example, light waves travel faster through air than through glass.

You've observed, with a spring toy and water, how waves transmit energy without transporting matter in the direction of the wave. But can you describe how energy moves through waves? In the next activity, you'll make a wave machine and use it to demonstrate what happens to the matter and energy in waves in a medium other than water.

frequency = 10 waves/minute   wavelength = 3m

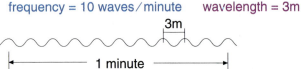

frequency = 20 waves/minute   wavelength = 3m

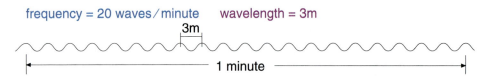

frequency = 30 waves/minute   wavelength = 1m

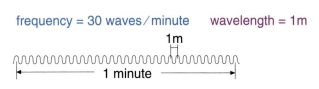

TRY THIS Activity!

Elastic Wave Machine

You can observe and describe how energy moves through waves.

What You Need

1 m of 2-cm-wide unstretched elastic
25 plastic drinking straws
staples, stapler
table
Activity Log page 7

1. Take a 1 m length of elastic and lay it across the table.
2. Lay the straws across the elastic like railroad ties at right angles to the elastic, with the same length of each straw sticking out on either side. The straws should be about a finger's width apart on the elastic.
3. Using the stapler, carefully staple each straw in place on the elastic. Make sure you staple each straw lengthwise as shown.
4. With a partner, pick the straw track up from the table and hold it between you, so the straws are positioned vertically in the air.
5. Grab and move the straws back and forth gently at one end. What happens? Now do the same thing from the other end. What do you see?

6. Now tap them more quickly.
7. Tap the two ends at the same time in opposite directions, then in the same direction. Watch carefully. What happens as the waves collide? Record your observations in your *Activity Log*.

In the previous activity, you made straw waves. It's easy to see the straws vibrating back and forth. But how is the wave motion actually transmitting energy?

When the first straw vibrates, it twists the elastic slightly. That twisting motion transfers the energy from the first straw to the next one. As the second straw vibrates, it twists the elastic and transmits energy to the third straw. This transmission of energy moves down the straw wave, but the straws stay in place. As you can observe, energy, not matter, has moved in the wave. You will use your straw wave machine later in this lesson and again in the next lesson to demonstrate other properties of waves.

21

Wave Interference

Waves are energy carriers. A soft breeze can send ripples across the surface of a puddle or lake. Ripples are tiny waves with the energy to bob a water bug up and down. Hurricane winds can build ocean waves the size of walls, waves powerful enough to toss ships and tear down lighthouses.

How do such powerful waves occur? Think back to the spring toy activity. When the crests of two waves pass a given point at the same time, they are "in phase" and the wave crests add to make each other stronger. However, if the crest of one wave passes a given point at the same time as the trough of the other wave, they become weaker. They are "out of phase" and "interfere" with one another, resulting in less wave height. If the crests of many waves come together at the same time, they are "in phase," resulting in more wave height. Water waves that are "in phase" can suddenly produce a huge wave called a "rogue" (rōg) wave. Rogue waves have been known to reach heights of 30 meters.

Rogue waves are freaks of the sea. They can seem to appear all of a sudden, out of nowhere in the middle of the ocean as the crests of several waves overlap in phase. Once the wave crests are out of phase, a rogue wave can disappear just as suddenly as it appeared.

This addition and subtraction of wave crests and troughs is called wave interference. All waves have wave interference. You can observe wave interference in the following activity.

Wave Interference

You can formulate models of waves to show how they are affected by interference.

What You Need

spring toy, safety goggles, meter tape, *Activity Log* page 8

1. You and your partner should each hold one end of the spring toy and stretch it across the floor to a length of 3 m. **Safety Tip:** Wear your goggles throughout this activity.
2. Each of you should make a transverse wave in the spring toy with a quick back-and-forth motion of your hands. Observe what happens to the waves as they pass each other.
3. Repeat step 2 until the waves make one large wave as they pass each other. Draw a diagram of what happens in your ***Activity Log***.
4. Repeat step 2 until the waves seem to disappear as they pass each other. Draw a diagram of what happens in your ***Activity Log***.
5. Correctly label the diagrams for steps 3 and 4 "in phase" and "out of phase," and explain these terms in your own words to describe the action of the waves.
6. Hypothesize ways you can use your straw wave machine from the previous activity to demonstrate wave interference. Record these ways in your ***Activity Log***.

Wave interference can sometimes be helpful. Engineers are using what they know about wave interference to make noisy electric generators quiet. They create artificially produced sound waves that are out of phase with the generator sounds in a way that the crests and troughs line up so the waves cancel each other out. The result is less noise and a much quieter environment. As you read on, you can find out how wave interference can make some buildings safer places to live and work.

Focus on Technology
"Smart Building"

Imagine living or working in a "smart building!" Smart buildings were developed in response to the need worldwide for buildings that can endure the massive amounts of energy carried by earthquake waves. These are waves that travel through Earth carrying the destructive energy of a wave. Engineers in the United States and Japan are developing control systems to be incorporated into the designs of some buildings that are located in areas of potential earthquakes. These "smart buildings" are capable of detecting and suppressing their own vibrations to minimize damage.

In addition to the wave energy supplied by earthquake waves, strong winds can make

If active or passive control systems had been installed when these buildings were constructed, the damage to them would not have been so great. Many lives might have been saved.

the top floors of skyscrapers sway several meters from their resting positions. This oscillating motion can make the people inside the top floors of these buildings feel sick and disoriented. During an earthquake, these buildings can sway back and forth with the same frequency of the earthquake waves traveling through Earth. The motion of the building caused by the wind can increase the energy of the earthquake waves if they have wave interference that is "in phase." This increased energy from the combined motions can cause the building to collapse!

Have you ever wondered how some buildings are designed to withstand earthquakes? Once buildings in earthquake-prone areas were designed with a "more is better" approach to safety. They were designed to be solid and inflexible and were made of massive, heavy materials. These buildings could withstand minor earthquake tremors but could still sustain damage during a major earthquake. Today, engineers and architects are trying a different approach to the problem by developing both active and passive control systems to be included in the structures of buildings as they are constructed in earthquake regions.

Active control systems, those requiring movement—long used on airplanes, boats, and spaceships—are also being incorporated into "smart buildings." Sensors, devices that

An Earthquake-safe Building

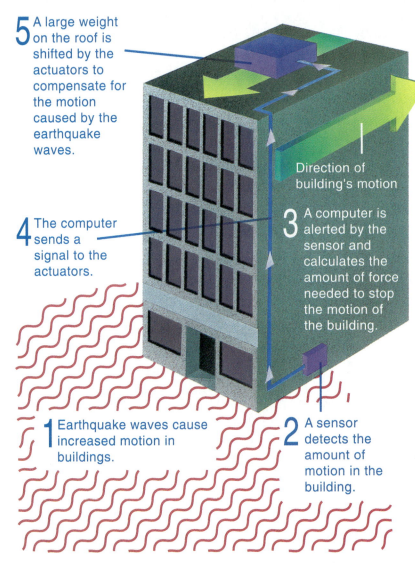

5 A large weight on the roof is shifted by the actuators to compensate for the motion caused by the earthquake waves.

4 The computer sends a signal to the actuators.

3 A computer is alerted by the sensor and calculates the amount of force needed to stop the motion of the building.

Direction of building's motion

1 Earthquake waves cause increased motion in buildings.

2 A sensor detects the amount of motion in the building.

respond to motion, are embedded in the foundation and walls and used to detect vibrations set off when the ground shakes or the wind blows. Some of these "smart sensors" even detect motion caused by outside traffic! The sensors relay information about motion to a computer. The computer calculates the force needed to eliminate the motion of the building caused by the wind and signals powerful hydraulic arms, called actuators. The actuators adjust the position of massive steel weights on the roof of the building and the swaying stops. Compare this active control system to the way you might shift your weight on skis or a skateboard to control your motion.

Another active control system involves using steel braces with sensors that are connected to computers. Conventional steel tubes that make up the framework of a building are fitted with actuators at each end. When the computer sends a warning signal, the actuators lengthen or shorten the building's internal braces to react to the motion without damaging the building. This motion can be compared to your body's reflex action when muscles either contract or lengthen in response to nerve impulses.

In California, another engineer is developing an active control system using jet thrusters, a type of engine, mounted on the roof. When sensors alert the computer, a signal is sent to power the thrusters. Compressed air is fired from these jets just long enough to stabilize the building.

Another way to control building motion is with a passive control system. Unlike the active control systems you just read about, passive control systems do not require the transfer of energy to filter out the shaking that results from earthquakes. Huge rubber pads under the foundations of buildings act like springs, or shock absorbers to absorb some of the destructive energy of earthquake waves so they will not be intense enough to harm the actual structure of the building. This same principle applies to the use of shock absorbers in automobiles and the use of thick rubber soles in running shoes.

Active and passive control systems will make new buildings more expensive. But the new technology may allow architects and engineers to design buildings that use fewer, lighter, and more flexible materials. These buildings will also be more durable against the effects of earthquake waves. Many new designs for "smart buildings" are still on the drawing board. Questions of reliability and cost must be addressed before this new technology becomes a routine part of building construction. However, where human lives are concerned, safety is the most important issue of all.

Sum It Up

In this lesson, you've discovered how some waves form and how they carry energy. You've examined how waves move through different media. You have seen that different types of waves share common characteristics, such as wavelength, frequency, and amplitude. With this knowledge, you should be able to explain to a friend how you're able to float on a raft in a pool without being swept away by passing waves. You should also be able to explain to your friend why waves are important. Without waves, we could not see light or hear sounds. It would be very difficult to transfer energy without waves.

Using Vocabulary

amplitude
crest
frequency
transverse wave
trough
wavelength

Use the vocabulary words in this lesson to describe the characteristics and actions of waves.

Critical Thinking

1. Draw a transverse wave and on it label these characteristics—crest, trough, and amplitude.
2. You are observing water waves. You notice that their amplitude increases, but their wavelength and frequency stay the same. What can you infer about these waves based on your observations?
3. Light waves carry energy through a medium in a way similar to water waves. Describe in which direction light waves carry energy.
4. How can you change the length of a wave without changing its speed?
5. Describe wave interference and tell which type results in more energy.

Theme **T** ENERGY

Quiet Out There!

Why are some sounds pleasing to the ear whereas others are not so pleasing? In this lesson you will describe different sounds by vibrations that transfer energy.

Think about the sounds in each of these scenes:

Try to recall each of the sounds represented in the photos on these two pages.

Are these sounds loud or soft?

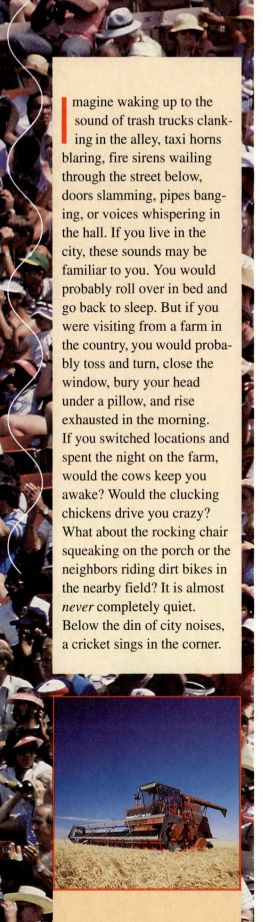

Imagine waking up to the sound of trash trucks clanking in the alley, taxi horns blaring, fire sirens wailing through the street below, doors slamming, pipes banging, or voices whispering in the hall. If you live in the city, these sounds may be familiar to you. You would probably roll over in bed and go back to sleep. But if you were visiting from a farm in the country, you would probably toss and turn, close the window, bury your head under a pillow, and rise exhausted in the morning. If you switched locations and spent the night on the farm, would the cows keep you awake? Would the clucking chickens drive you crazy? What about the rocking chair squeaking on the porch or the neighbors riding dirt bikes in the nearby field? It is almost *never* completely quiet. Below the din of city noises, a cricket sings in the corner. Above the soft stirrings of a barnyard, a bird sings overhead.

Minds On! Think about the sounds in your school. Where are the best places to study? Where do you like to talk with your friends? What are the differences between those places? In your *Activity Log* page 9, make two columns—one for a noisy place in your school; and one for a quiet place. Predict the types of sounds you might hear in those two places and record them in your *Activity Log* page 9.

Go to the contrasting sound locations you have picked. What do you hear compared to the sounds you predicted you would hear? Are there more sounds than you expected in each place, or fewer? Return to your classroom. In your *Activity Log* page 9, write down the sounds you actually heard. How would you react to a sound from the loud environment if it occurred in the quiet place you observed? Would you be able to detect a sound from the quiet location if it occurred in the loud environment?

Sounds fill your world every day. What sounds are familiar in your sound environment? What sounds would be out of place?

Perceptions of sounds change in different locations and situations. You can sharpen a pencil in your school cafeteria at noon without being detected. If you tried to dribble a basketball through the library, however, someone might be startled! Your sound environment affects your ability (or inability) to tolerate background sounds and noises.

Sound waves, like water waves and light waves, transmit energy. Wind sets most water waves in motion. See if you can determine the cause or source of sound waves in this next activity.

Why do you think we hear sounds?

What do sounds have to do with waves?

Are sound waves the same kind of waves as water waves?

EXPLORE Activity!

How Are Sounds Produced?

You have been thinking about sounds and what causes them. As you have seen, there are many kinds and sources of sounds. Despite their differences, all sounds have one thing in common—what causes them.

What You Need

a thick tuning fork
wooden ruler
rubber bands (various sizes and thicknesses)
empty soup can with both ends removed (no sharp edges)
large piece of rubber
small piece of a mirror (about 1 or 2 cm on a side, the edges covered with tape)
transparent tape
flashlight
Activity Log pages 10–11

What To Do

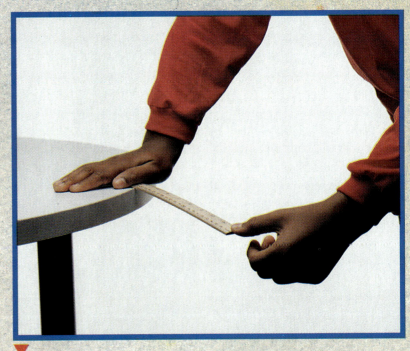

1 Hold the ruler firmly against a table so that more than half of it hangs over the end. Pull the end of the ruler down and then let it go. What do you notice? Do you hear any sound? What do you see the ruler doing while it is making a sound? Record all observations in your **Activity Log**.

2. Strike the tuning fork against the bottom of your shoe or something else that is firm. (Do not strike it against anything hard like a wooden desk, as this could damage the tuning fork, the desk, or both.) Bring the tuning fork near your ear. What do you hear? Look at the ends of the tuning fork. What do you see? Make a sketch in your **Activity Log** of what it looks like.

3. Now, carefully stretch a rubber band and have your partner pluck it like a guitar string. Do you hear a sound? Look closely at the rubber band after it is plucked. What does it look like? How does it compare to the ends of the tuning fork when it is struck? Now, try rubber bands of different sizes. Do you notice anything different about the sounds they produce?

4. Stretch the piece of rubber over one end of the soup can and fasten it in place with a rubber band. Tape the small mirror to the rubber. The mirror should be slightly off center as shown in the picture.

5. One member of your group should shine a light on the mirror so a reflection can be seen on the wall or the ceiling. Now talk or sing into the open end of the can. You will have to hold the can firmly against your face. Sing or speak loudly and clearly. What happens to the reflection on the wall? What patterns do you see? What is causing them? Record all observations in your **Activity Log**.

What Happened?

1. What seemed to cause the sounds you heard in each part of the activity? How was each one alike?
2. What examples of vibrating objects did you observe in this activity?
3. How is sound production related to vibrations?

What Now?

1. Perhaps you have felt the beat of loud music. What were you actually feeling?
2. How is sound produced by a guitar similar to that produced by the rubber band in this activity? How is sound produced with a violin when it is bowed?
3. How do you think other musical instruments produce sounds?

EXPLORE

Communicating With Sound

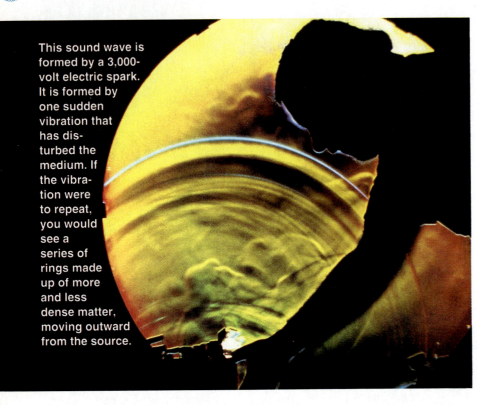

This sound wave is formed by a 3,000-volt electric spark. It is formed by one sudden vibration that has disturbed the medium. If the vibration were to repeat, you would see a series of rings made up of more and less dense matter, moving outward from the source.

In the Explore Activity using the tuning fork, the rubber band, and ruler, you observed that all sounds are produced by movements or vibrations (vī-brā′shəns). **Vibrations** are back-and-forth movements of matter. The vibrations set sound waves in motion. As the sound waves move away from their vibrating source, they transmit energy in all directions. Think about common sounds you hear at school or at home. What are the sources of vibrations of these sounds?

When you ring a bell, the clapper strikes the inside surface and makes the bell vibrate. If you put your hand on the bell, you stop the vibrations and the bell is quiet. No sound is produced. You strum a chord on a guitar and decide you've hit the wrong notes. All you have to do to stop the sound is press your hand on top of the strings to stop the vibrations. No vibration means no sound.

People make all kinds of sounds. Fans at football games yell cheers or jeers loud enough to carry across a stadium. A drowsy baby sleeps while a voice hums a soft lullaby. Variations are endless as people whisper, whistle, sing, and talk throughout each day.

People aren't the only living creatures to communicate using sound. Can you think of some animals that might communicate with sounds? Have you ever been to a whale show at an aquarium? Killer whales leap into the air in graceful arcs with water spraying from their blowholes. As they rise, they screech and whistle like gigantic balloons letting out air. The whales are communicating with sound. Crickets rub their wings together. Howler monkeys can be heard for miles through rain forests. Wolves bay at the moon. Some fish even grunt at one another with organs called swim bladders located below their backbones. Animals depend on the ability to communicate —*Food is here. Danger is there. Notice me. Go away.* These are types of messages used for survival, and these messages are sent with sound.

A symphony orchestra uses instruments of wood and brass to fill a concert hall with smooth, rich tones. A rock concert electronically amplifies music with nerve-jangling, heart-pumping beats. When you were younger, you and your friends may have formed a neighborhood band using a spoon, a cup, a tissue, and comb. What is at the root of this endless symphony of sounds in the world? The answer is the same for them all!

Producing Sound

A well-known question asks, "If a tree falls in the forest and no one is there to hear it, does it make a sound?" What do you think?

What You Need
tuning fork, container of water, *Activity Log* page 12

Strike a tuning fork against something firm. Hold it to your ear and listen. Strike the tuning fork again and immediately place it in a small container of water. Observe what happens. What is being transmitted through the water? Record these observations in your *Activity Log*.

Now, can you predict what would happen if a tree were to fall in the forest and there was no one present? When you sing, your vocal cords vibrate, sending sound waves into the air. When you beat on a drum, its membrane vibrates. Sound waves in the air make your eardrum vibrate, and it sends a signal to your brain. This is how you "hear" sounds.

Sometimes objects can be damaged by too much vibration. Extremely loud sounds can cause your eardrum to vibrate too much and tear. You know that if you thump a glass with your finger, it will vibrate and produce a ringing sound. If the glass is caused to vibrate too much—possibly by a singer singing a note of a particular frequency—the glass could crack and shatter.

Minds On! Think of the instruments in a brass band or orchestra. Think about how they are played. What sounds do they make? Try to figure out what is vibrating as each creates its distinctive musical sound.

The wind can cause a bridge to vibrate, represented by the wave at the top. Traffic moving over a bridge can cause it to vibrate also, represented by the middle wave. If these vibrations were added together "in phase," the resulting wave could carry enough energy to cause the entire bridge to collapse.

31

Action of Sound Waves

Have you ever tossed a pebble into a pond? Water waves move away in rings from the impact point of the pebble. Recall the waves that formed when you placed the vibrating tuning fork in water. In a pond, small floating objects, like leaves or sticks, bob up and down as the wave moves under them. As you observed in the previous lesson, water waves are modeled by transverse waves. Recall how the matter vibrated up and down, or side to side, as the energy moved forward along the wave. Sound waves move in a different way. The disturbance to the medium moves in the same direction as the sound wave. In other words, the matter moves back and forth as the energy moves forward along the wave. Sound waves are a type of wave known as a **longitudinal** (lon′ji tü′də nəl) **wave.**

The compressional part of a longitudinal wave, which is called the compression, is the crest. The expanded part of a longitudinal wave, called the rarefaction, is the trough. The wavelength of the longitudinal wave is the distance from one point of a wave to the identical part of the next wave.

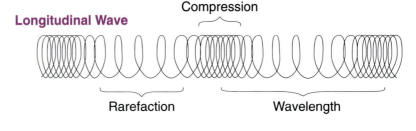

Longitudinal Wave

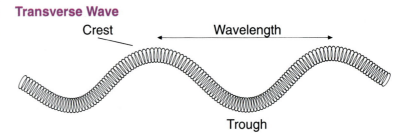

Transverse Wave

What Wave Is This?

Recall the transverse waves you made with the spring toy and the straw wave machine in a previous lesson. You can now model longitudinal waves with these same objects.

What You Need

spring toy, straw wave machine, meter tape, goggles, *Activity Log* **page 13**

Put on your goggles. Then have one partner hold one end of the spring as you stretch it across the floor a distance of 3 m. Now, pinch a few of the coils together and quickly release them. Observe the wave that you created. How does the spring toy transfer energy in relationship to the transverse wave you made in the spring toy in the last lesson?

Next, make a longitudinal wave with the straw wave machine from the last lesson. Slightly stretch the elastic between yourself and a partner. Turn the elastic so the straws are vertical. Pinch the first few straws together and quickly release them. Describe how the energy moves along this wave in relationship to the direction the matter moves as it vibrates. Using the spring toy or the straw wave machine, investigate what happens to the longitudinal waves when you put more energy into them. Record all observations in your *Activity Log*.

Like water waves, sound waves require a medium in which to travel. They can transmit energy through solids, liquids, and gases (for example, wood, glass, steel, water, air). How do sounds change when you listen underwater in a bathtub or pool? Why does distant talking and laughing seem closer underwater? If you were on a boat on the ocean and witnessed an explosion far away in the water, you'd hear two loud booms! This would happen because the sound would travel through the water and through the air at different speeds. Have you ever listened to voices from the floor below by putting your ear on a radiator in an old house? Sound carries nearly 15 times faster through metal than air.

The speed of sound waves varies with the medium. Generally, sound travels faster in solids than liquids, and faster in liquids than gases. This is because sound waves travel faster in more dense media. Recall that of solids, liquids, and gases, the atoms in solids are more densely arranged than those in liquids; those in liquids are more densely packed than those in gases. In other words, the more closely the particles are packed together, the less distance they need to vibrate in transferring energy to the next particle.

The Ewe (eh′ vay) drummers of Africa use drums that have strings stretched from top to bottom all around them to send different sounds through the air. Ewe drummers "talk" to their people many miles away by squeezing the strings against their bodies as they hit the drums. This makes the sound higher or lower.

Native Americans made practical use of this property of sound. By putting their ears to the ground, they were able to locate buffalo herds. The sound of the stampeding hooves could be heard through the solid ground long before the sound could be heard through the air. This confirms that sounds can be heard through solids at greater distances than through the air.

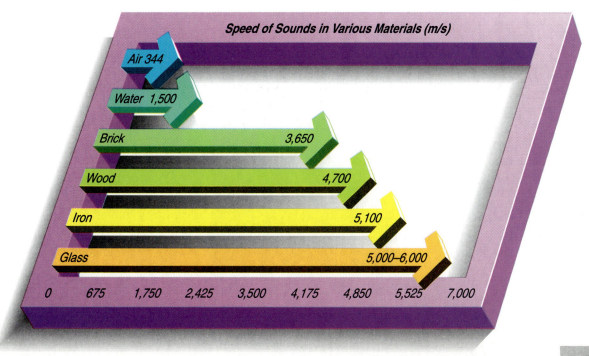

Speed of Sounds in Various Materials (m/s)

- Air 344
- Water 1,500
- Brick 3,650
- Wood 4,700
- Iron 5,100
- Glass 5,000–6,000

Sound in Your Environment

Have you ever noticed that during a thunderstorm you rarely hear the crash of the thunder at the same time that you see the flash of the lightning that produced the sound wave? That's because the lightning usually occurs several kilometers away, and the light waves reach you before the sound waves do. The light waves reach you first because they travel almost one million times faster through air than sound waves do! You can use this information to estimate how far away lightning occurs.

Timing Sound

Sound travels through air at about 344 meters (1,128 feet) per second. Imagine you have hiked to a mountain valley for a picnic. Clouds move in. Lightning flashes far off in the sky. The sound of its crack does not reach you for 14 seconds. How far away is the lightning?

Focus on Environment

Noise Pollution

If there were two empty seats at a rock concert, one directly below a gigantic speaker on the stage, and one in the very last row of the auditorium, which seat would you choose? Why? Sounds can be comfortable or painful depending on the nearness and loudness of the sound source.

When does sound become noise? Noises are unpleasant and distracting sounds. Could you concentrate on your homework if a two-year-old child was making motor noises with a toy truck beside your desk? Banging trash can lids, barking dogs, lawn mowers, and vacuum cleaners

34

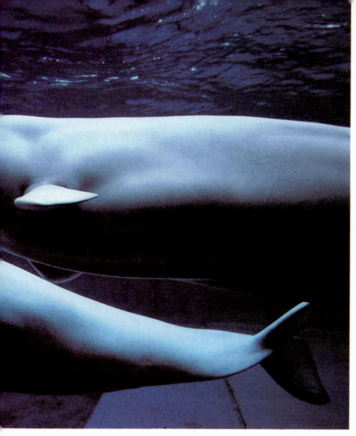

Beluga whales use sound waves in the water to communicate with other members of their species.

are all noisemakers. When a vibrating object sends out irregular vibrations at irregular intervals, it makes noise. Nature creates plenty of noise. Earth rumbles with destructive seismic waves. Lightning produces violent vibrations in heated air, and we hear thunder. People who have experienced tornadoes have compared the sound of a tornado to that of a thundering train.

We all experience noise daily. Maybe you wake up each day to the sounds of hammers banging and electric saws buzzing as construction workers are building a new structure on your street. Perhaps your parents work in a factory or an airport. These places can be quite noisy because of the huge engines that can be found there. Even the rest of us are guilty of contributing a little to environmental noise every day. Think of the noises you make when you ride your skateboard or slam your metal locker door shut.

Constant exposure to noise, even noises that are not extremely loud, can cause tiredness, headaches, hearing loss, irritability, nausea, and nervousness. Scientists are discovering that people are not the only organisms that can be harmed by noise pollution.

Marine mammals, like seals and whales, have extremely sensitive hearing. Evidence suggests that the noise of underwater blasting and drilling, and the impact of icebreaker ship hulls on pack ice can damage their hearing. Some marine mammals, such as beluga whales, rely on their keen sense of hearing for safety. For example, these whales emit distress calls to other belugas when an icebreaker is 80 kilometers (50 miles) away, and they will flee the area before the ship is within 40 kilometers (25 miles).

Obviously, we must somehow control the noise in our environment. Some local governments have created laws to try to do this. These laws recognize certain kinds of noise as noise pollution, depending on how loud they are and where they are located. Can you imagine having to pay a fine because you broke a law by making too much noise? The federal government is also involved in monitoring noise pollution. One federal agency, the Occupational Safety and Health Administration (OSHA), is largely concerned with the effects of loud noises on employees in some working environments. OSHA requires workers in some noisy places to wear protective devices to reduce the amount of noise entering their ears. Thanks to the efforts of acoustic engineers, we are learning to control the damaging effects of noise in our environment.

Minds On! What devices and inventions are improving your sound environment? Hypothesize ways to improve a noisy area in your home, school, or neighborhood. Record them in your *Activity Log* page 14. Then, try one out at home and see if it works.

35

Some sounds are annoying to us while others are pleasing. Some sound is used in some ways that help us advance technologically in many areas. One area of advancement is the use of sound in the fishing industry.

Have you ever waited for hours in a rowboat hoping to catch a fish, only to discover the worm bait still on your hook? You feel a tug and yank on the line and nothing appears but the bait! You hang over the side of the boat squinting through the surface glare, trying to spot the elusive fish below you.

Fishing With Sonar

A hundred miles off the coast of Bermuda, Charlie Vieira sits on the deck of his fishing boat searching for fish. He is not baiting lines or hanging over the railing. Charlie is scanning the water hundreds of meters below by watching his sonar screen.

The word *sonar* comes from the words *S*ound *N*avigation *A*nd *R*anging. Sonar devices use sound waves to locate underwater objects and to determine the depths of water beneath the ship. Charlie's sonar device sends a sharp pulse of sound down into the water below his boat. This steady "ping...ping...ping" is reflected back when it hits the seafloor. It also reflects back when it hits a school of fish. The fish will appear on the sonar screen as a band between his boat and the seafloor.

The distance to the fish is determined by measuring the time it takes for the sonar ping to return to the boat. Sound travels through water at a speed of about 1,540 meters (5,000 feet) per second. If Charlie hears an echo after three seconds, the sound has traveled 4,614 meters (15,000 feet)—2,307 meters (7,500 feet) down and 2,307 meters back. Now Charlie knows how far down his nets must be lowered to capture a good haul of fish.

This method of measuring distance is called echo ranging.

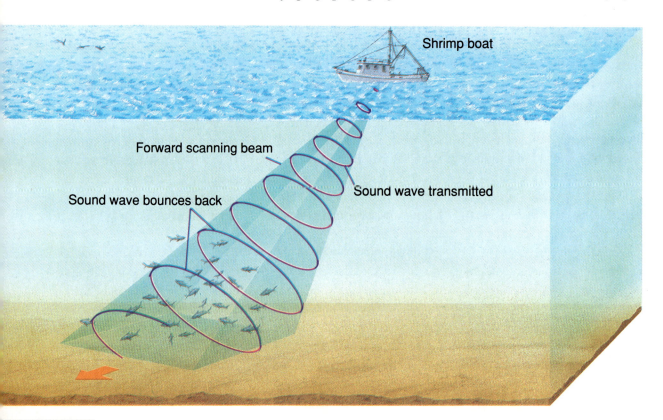

Charlie is using sonar echo ranging to make his living as a fisherman. Airplanes and ships use sonar to detect submarines. Salvage companies use it to locate sunken treasures. Bats and dolphins navigate with a natural sonar system called echolocation that enables them to know the distance between them and objects that may obstruct their paths or the distance to their prey.

The use of sonar has made Charlie Vieira's job much easier because he can now locate large schools of fish quickly. As a result, he can catch more fish than he did before he used echo ranging to find them. As you can see, sonar echo ranging has applications in helping us locate objects or distances to those objects even though we can't see them.

Sum It Up

In this lesson, you studied the sounds in your everyday world. You observed that sounds are perceived differently in different locations and situations. People and animals rely on sound for communication. Sound waves are produced by vibrations that transmit energy through a medium. The speed of sound varies with the medium through which it travels. Generally, sounds travel faster in solids than liquids, and faster in liquids than gases. The comfort and quality of your sound environment is important to your health and hearing. It may also be important to your creativity and productivity.

Using Vocabulary

longitudinal wave
vibrations

Using the vocabulary words *vibrations* and *longitudinal wave* as key words, write a paragraph that includes these two definitions but also explains the relationship of vibrations to longitudinal waves. Include examples to illustrate your paragraphs. Check your paragraph for introductory statement, development, and conclusion. Be sure to proofread for sense, spelling, and punctuation.

Critical Thinking

1. Describe the type of media sound waves need to transfer energy, and infer how the nature of each medium affects the sound waves.
2. What must occur for a sound to be produced?
3. How could two astronauts communicate on the moon?
4. Compare and contrast longitudinal and transverse waves.
5. What could be happening in a place where there is no sound being produced?

Theme **T** ENERGY

What Is That Strange Sound?

The chirping of a bird...the rustling of leaves...are familiar sounds in our environment. In this lesson you will explore the energy of sound that gives each vibration its own distinct characteristic.

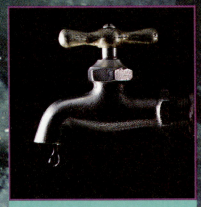

Think about the sound of a single drop of water.

Think about the sound of an enormous waterfall. What is the difference between the two?

Have you listened to waves crashing on a beach?

You step into a movie theater and a familiar smell hits you right away. No doubt about it...popcorn! If your friends blindfolded you and fed you some, you could still identify it as popcorn by its taste and smell. What about sounds? If you heard popcorn popping, without being able to smell it or taste it, would you know what it was?

What makes sounds familiar? You recognize which friend is on the telephone after just one word is spoken, "Hi." Why do rustling sounds in your classroom alert you to the fact that the bell is about to ring?

Have you ever gone to a zoo? Think of the zoo sounds you might have heard. Can you recall how monkeys chatter as they dangle from the bars of their cage? A lion lets out a thunderous roar as it paces back and forth. Peacocks spread their glorious fans of feathers and screech unexpectedly. If you closed your eyes, could you tell which part of the zoo you were in by the sounds? But what if the elephants chattered? What if the reptiles roared?

Minds On! Work with a partner. Take turns sitting blindfolded in a chair while the other person makes sounds by opening a drawer, flipping the pages of a book, sharpening a pencil, tapping a pen, crinkling paper. Use your imagination. Make sounds with anything you can think of around the room and see if you can stump your partner as he or she tries to hypothesize the sources of the sounds. What sound was the most unusual? Could you identify it? How did you identify it? Did you have to have your partner repeat any sounds before you could determine what they were? Why do you think some sounds were more difficult to identify than others? Record what happened on page 15 in your *Activity Log.*

Making sense of sounds, recognizing them, and identifying them helps you navigate your way safely through each day. You recognize the sound of an approaching car, so you don't step into the street. You hear your alarm clock ring and get up on time for school. A buzz from the microwave means your snack is cooked. We respond almost automatically to the sounds around us.

How do you recognize sounds so clearly? The everyday sounds of life are familiar because you hear them over and over. But what makes each sound distinctive?

What other sounds can you associate with water?

How do you distinguish the sounds of rippling water waves from the thunderous crash of waves hitting a sea cliff?

What sounds do you think of when you look at this photograph?

39

EXPLORE Activity!

Making Sounds With Bottles

You've been identifying sounds based on some of their characteristics. One characteristic of sound is the way you can hear a change in the frequency of sound waves. You are going to make a mock xylophone using water and soft drink bottles and predict how the sounds will change as a result of adjusting the amount of water in the bottles.

What You Need

6 tall glass soft drink bottles
pencil
water
***Activity Log* pages 16–17**

What To Do

1. Get 6 empty soft drink bottles. Strike one bottle below the neck with a pencil and notice the sound it makes. Hypothesize what is vibrating.

3. Predict what will happen to the highness or lowness of the sounds as you add different amounts of water to the bottles. Record this prediction in your *Activity Log*.

2. Add a little water to one of the bottles. Tap it again in the same place you tapped it in step 1 and compare the sound it makes to that of an empty bottle. Is the sound higher or lower? Record the results in your *Activity Log*.

4. Add different amounts of water to the bottles and tap each bottle with your pencil. Were your predictions in step 3 correct?

5. Try to compose a song with your soft-drink-bottle xylophone.

6 Blow across the top of an empty bottle and notice the highness or lowness of the sound produced. Hypothesize what *two* things could have changed to produce this sound. Why do you think the highness or lowness of the sound changed?

7 Now blow across the top of a bottle that has some water in it. Notice the highness or lowness of the sound. How does it compare to the sound produced by the empty bottle?

8 You have created another instrument with different characteristics! Try to make a scale and compose a song by blowing across the tops of the bottles. Record your composition in your *Activity Log*.

What Happened?

1. Which bottle made the highest sound when struck with a pencil? Which made the lowest sound?
2. Which bottle made the highest sound when you blew across the top? The lowest? Why do you think this happened?
3. What vibrated to produce the sounds when you hit the bottles with a pencil and when you blew across the tops of the bottles?

What Now?

1. On a real xylophone, sounds are produced on metal bars. Do you think the metal bars producing the high sounds are small or large? Why?
2. Why do you think men's voices usually sound lower than women's? What can you hypothesize about the size of a man's vocal cords as compared to those of a woman?
3. When you fill a glass of water or a bottle, you may notice that as you fill it, the sound changes. Does it become higher or lower? Why?
4. Answer all questions and record all observations in your *Activity Log*.

EXPLORE

Properties of Sound

Two basic characteristics of sound are pitch and loudness. **Pitch** is simply the highness or lowness of a sound as we perceive it. When you added different levels of water to the bottles in the activity, you were changing the amounts of water and air that vibrated so that you heard different pitches. Think about the pitch of a low blast of a foghorn, or the high sweet song of a canary. The foghorn produces sound waves with a low pitch and frequency. The canary produces sound waves with a high pitch. Think about the pitch of sounds you hear daily. Which sounds have the highest pitch and which ones have the lowest pitch?

Remember the waves you produced along a spring toy in Lesson 1? As you moved your wrist faster, the number of waves along the spring increased and the distance between each wave decreased. Sound waves work the same way. Low-frequency sounds produce fewer waves per second. As a result, you hear a low sound. Likewise, high-frequency waves produce many waves per second, and you hear a high sound.

As you can see, the pitch of a sound you hear is related to its frequency. As the pitch rises, the frequency of the sound waves increases. As the pitch falls, the frequency of the sound waves decreases. The relationship between frequency and pitch is simple and direct. High-pitched sounds have a high frequency; low-pitched sounds have a low frequency.

Were you surprised by your observations in the activity with the bottles on pages 40–41? As

500 B.C.

400 B.C.

1 The study of sound dates back to ancient Greece. A Greek philosopher and mathematician, Pythagoras (pi thag′ ər əs), investigated sounds produced by vibrating strings as early as 500 B.C.

2 About one hundred years later (about 400 B.C.), Archytas (är′ kit äs), a Greek scholar, hypothesized that sound can be produced by the motion of one object hitting another. The Greek philosopher Aristotle (ar′ ə stot′ əl), about 350 B.C., proposed that sound is transferred to our ears by the motion of air.

3 Between 475-221 B.C., the Chinese knew that there was a relationship between the tension of a string and its pitch by observing that atmospheric humidity affects the tension of stringed instruments. The Chinese observed that increased humidity loosened the strings, creating a different musical note than when the air was less humid.

you filled the bottles with water and tapped them, the pitch of the sounds produced dropped. But when you filled the bottles with water and blew over the tops, the pitch of the sounds rose. The empty bottle had the highest pitch when tapped and the lowest pitch when you blew across the top!

Why does this turnabout take place? When you tap an empty bottle, you set off a sound wave by making the bottle vibrate. But as you add water to the bottle, you increase its mass. Both the bottle *and* the water must vibrate to produce sound. As the bottle fills with water, it vibrates more slowly. When the frequency of vibrations decreases, the pitch drops and you hear a lower sound.

When you blow across an empty bottle, you vibrate the air column in the bottle. When the bottle is empty, the air column is longest and the vibrations are slow. As you add water to the bottle, the air column grows shorter. As a result, the number of vibrations per second increases. When the frequency rises, the pitch rises and you hear a higher sound. The following activity will help you observe the relationship between frequency and pitch.

4 Four hundred years ago Galileo, the great Italian astronomer, explored the relationship between pitch and frequency in sound waves.

A.D. 1600

A.D. 1901

5 In 1901, Guglielmo Marconi, an Italian inventor and electrical engineer, transmitted the first transatlantic wireless communication.

TRY THIS Activity!

Frequency and Pitch

Have you ever noticed the change in sound of a bicycle wheel as it increases in speed? Predict what you think will happen.

What You Need
several playing cards
bicycle
Activity Log page 18

Attach a card to a bicycle wheel so that it makes a clicking sound on the spokes as the wheel turns. As the wheel turns, every passing spoke will bend and flip the card producing a flapping sound. Spin the wheel of the bicycle several times, increasing the speed of the spin each time. What happens to the pitch of the sound produced as the wheel turns faster? Relate your observations to frequency and pitch and write an explanation in your *Activity Log*.

Measuring Sound Frequency

Sound frequencies can be measured. To do this, we use a unit called a hertz (hûrts). One hertz equals one vibration (or cycle) per second. The abbreviation for hertz is Hz.

The unit is named after Heinrich Hertz, 1857–1894, who is known for his work with electromagnetic waves.

Sound frequencies generated by a dog whistle are too high to be detected by humans, but can be detected by dogs.

Think about the activity you just did with the card and the bicycle wheel. If ten spokes hit the card every second when you spun it, what was the frequency of the sound waves produced? How many times did the card snap per second? If you answered that the frequency is 10 hertz, and that you would hear the card snap ten times in a second, you were correct. Can you predict the frequency of the sound waves that would be produced if you doubled the speed of the spinning wheel?

Humans do not hear all sound waves but can hear sounds that range between 20 and 20,000 hertz (20 to 20,000 vibrations per second). As people grow older, their ears change and they are less able to hear higher-pitched sounds—10,000 hertz is a common upper limit for older people. Because of the design of their ears, dogs have a much broader range of hearing. Dogs are able to perceive sounds with frequencies as high as 50,000 hertz. Dog whistles are

designed to take advantage of this difference in hearing range. Dog whistles emit sounds at frequencies too high to be heard by humans. Dogs can hear the whistle, but we are not bothered by the sound it makes. Bats also have extremely sensitive ears, and are able to perceive sounds as high as 100,000 hertz!

Not all the sounds you hear are pleasant ones. A car backfires and hurts your ears. Fireworks on the Fourth of July are spectacular to behold, but hard on your hearing if you are too close to them when they explode. What hurts your ears? Is it the pitch? No, it is not the pitch that bothers you, but another property of sound, loudness. Do the activity on this page to find out what makes sounds louder.

TRY THIS Activity!

Making Louder Sounds

Using a rubber band, you can demonstrate how to make louder sounds and predict changes in the amplitude and frequency of the vibration.

What You Need
large rubber band, safety goggles, metric ruler, *Activity Log* page 19

Obtain a large rubber band that is about 5 mm wide. Have a partner hold the rubber band as shown. Grasp the top portion of the rubber band, pull it up about 2 cm from its original position, let it go, and observe what happens. Be careful not to change the wavelength. You have just created a sound by vibrating the rubber band. You can assume that the wave on the band models the sound wave that you produced. Next, predict what will happen to the amplitude and frequency of the sound wave if you pull the rubber band up 5 cm and release it. Write your prediction in your *Activity Log* and then try it. Was your prediction correct? What happened to the intensity, or loudness, of the sound as you increased the amplitude of the wave? How is loudness related to the energy the wave carries?

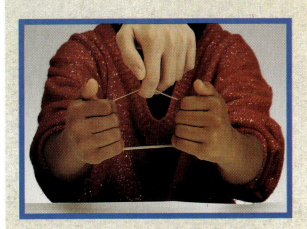

What happened to the sound that was produced when you pulled the rubber band up higher or with more energy? You probably noticed that the sounds you produced were more intense or sounded louder. **Loudness** is our perception of the intensity of a sound as it reaches our ears. Loudness, then, is related to the intensity of a sound wave. In addition, the more intense a sound is, the more energy it carries as it moves along. The intensity of a sound depends on the amplitude of the vibration that produced it.

Amplitude is the distance that a vibrating object moves from its rest position when it vibrates. Remember the amplitude of the coiled spring in Lesson 1? The more energy put into the vibration of the spring that created the transverse wave, the greater the amplitude of the wave. In sound waves, the larger the amplitude, the greater the intensity of the sound.

Amplitude is much like swinging on a swing set. When you were younger, you probably found that the harder you pumped your legs, the higher you rose from the swing's rest position—the straight-up-and-down position of the swing when no one is on it. When you swung up to the highest point

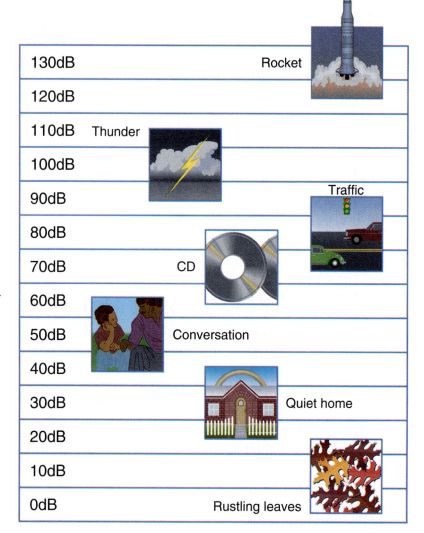

away from the rest position, you had the greatest energy and the highest amplitude.

If someone were to have walked in front of you while you were sitting on the swing, barely moving, nothing much would have happened if you'd bumped into each other. But if that person had walked in front of you just as you came hurtling down from your highest swing, you might have knocked that person across the playground and yourself off the swing! This would

happen because the amount of energy transferred to the other person in the second case was much greater than in the first.

Likewise, high energy sound waves have high intensity. Low energy sound waves have low intensity. Think again about the loudness of sound. How would you measure loudness? Loudness is measured in units called decibels (des′ ə belz), or dB. The loudness of sounds can be measured on a scale using these units. Zero on this scale is

Airline ground crews are required to wear ear protectors to muffle the intensity of sound waves that reach their ears.

known as the threshold of hearing—the lowest intensity sound that can be heard by an average person.

Remember the different sounds you heard in Lesson 2? Some sounds were heard in quiet places and some were heard in noisy places. It was your perception of the intensity of those sound waves that you perceived as loudness.

Normal conversation is about 65 decibels. An indoor rock concert may be as loud as 120 decibels, which is also the pain threshold for most people. Each increase of 10 decibels on the scale is 10 times louder. For example, a sound of 20 decibels (a whisper) is 10 times louder than a sound of 10 decibels (rustling leaves) and 100 times louder than the hearing threshold of 0 decibels! In the same way, a 40-decibel sound (quiet background music) is 1,000 times louder than those 10-decibel rustling leaves (10 × 10 × 10 = 1,000). This is important because when individuals are exposed to loud noises over an extended period of time, they may suffer temporary or permanent hearing loss. Think back to Lesson 2 when you compared the sounds in a quiet place with those in a noisy place. Look at the descriptions of those sounds that you wrote in your *Activity Log* on page 9. Why is it important to know about the decibel level around us? Can you predict where each sound should be placed on the decibel scale?

A Focus on Sound

You read in this lesson that music at indoor rock concerts can be as loud as the pain threshold for many people. Maybe that's where the idea came from that older people don't like loud music. They may only be concerned about the damage that can be caused to a person's hearing by listening to music at 120 decibels or louder. "If it's too loud, you're too old!" one rock musician used to bellow to his audiences.

Now some rock musicians are changing their minds about loud music. Many rock musicians are now experiencing some degree of hearing loss as a result of long periods of exposure to music that is too loud. Some are even speaking out and warning others of the problem.

Focus on Environment
Hold the Noise!

Pete Townshend of the rock group The Who is probably the most outspoken entertainer on the issue of loud music and hearing loss. For the last few years, Townshend has suffered from tinnitus (tin ī′ təs), a form of deafness that results in painful ringing in the ears. Billy Joel, another professional singer, makes his young daughter wear earmuff-styled earplugs when

Rock musician Pete Townshend has experienced hearing loss.

she attends his concerts. Most of his crew wear them, too.

You may not attend rock concerts. If that's the case, then loud music can't hurt you, right? **WRONG!** Many home and car stereos can play in the 110-decibel range, or even higher. If you listen to music at these levels of volume for long periods of time, you could damage your hearing.

Suppose you have a portable CD player that you listen to with earphones. Do you think those tiny earphones can damage your hearing? As a matter of fact, they can. Even the least expensive sets of headphones on the market can produce sounds in the 110-decibel range. More expensive ones may produce even louder sounds.

How can you tell if you are experiencing music or noise that is too loud? Should you purchase a sound level meter and carry it with you everywhere you go, just in case? No, that's not necessary. Instead, you should follow some simple guidelines for determining if noises are too loud. If you're listening to loud music or if you are in a very loud place, you should be able to carry on a conversation with a person standing one meter away *without having to yell.* If you have to yell to be heard, then you are being exposed to sounds that are too loud. Also, if you're wearing headphones and have the volume so loud that your parent or a friend has to yell at you to be heard over the music, then the music is too loud. You should avoid being in situations like these, where the sounds are intense enough to damage your hearing.

How can you tell if your hearing has already been damaged? Sometimes your ears seem to "ring" after you have been exposed to loud noises. Another symptom you can experience is "dulled" hearing. If you experience one or both of these symptoms, you probably have had some damage to your hearing. The damage may be only temporary and your hearing can return to normal. Excessive exposure to loud noises, however, can cause permanent damage to your hearing.

Knowing about loud noises and how they can affect your hearing, may change your opinion about how you like to listen to your favorite music. Next time you listen, think about the warning signs you just read about and, if necessary, turn the volume down a little.

Can you imagine a world without sound? Some people are deprived of the wonderful world of sound, but thanks to modern technology, many hearing-impaired people use electronic hearing aids to amplify sound.

Focus on Technology
Let There Be Sound!

Like a telephone, a hearing aid has a microphone, an amplifier, and a transmitter. The microphone receives sound waves and changes them into electrical impulses that are made stronger by the amplifier. These amplified impulses are sent to the transmitter, which changes them back into sound waves of greater amplitude or loudness.

Hearing aids are effective only for people with hearing loss that includes disorders of the outer or middle ear that prevent sound from reaching receptors in the inner ear. There is no nerve damage involved.

Depending on the type of hearing aid, sound waves are sent either directly to the inner ear or to the bone behind the ear. The cochlea (kōk′ lē ə), a spiral tube inside the inner ear, changes the sound waves into electrical signals and sends them to the brain. The brain interprets the signals and the sound is "heard."

Hearing aids may not be very effective when the person suffers from nerve-related hearing loss. This type of deafness results from damaged sensory hair cells that line the cochlea of the inner ear. A person having this disorder suffers a decreased sensitivity to sound and its interpretation.

Cochlear implants are becoming common practice to help those suffering from nerve-related hearing loss. These sensory hair cells are responsible for changing sound vibrations into nerve impulses.

In a cochlear implant, electrodes are used to replace the damaged sensory hair cells. In the most common type of device, a small battery-powered speech processor is attached to the person's belt or shirt pocket. This processor selects and converts different sounds from low frequencies to high frequencies. Coded digital signals are then relayed to the implanted electrodes in the cochlea by radio frequency transmission. Is this the most effective way to process sound for persons with hearing loss? Researchers are still struggling with this question.

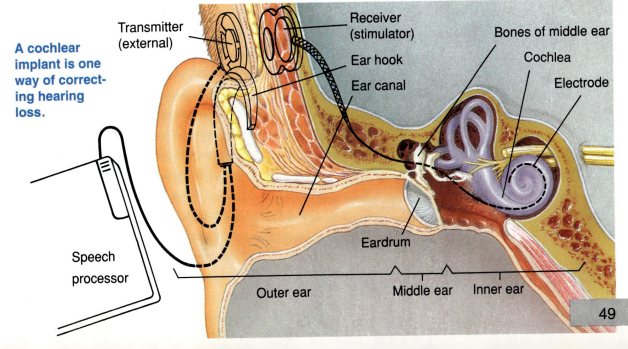

A cochlear implant is one way of correcting hearing loss.

We live with sound each day. Sound is a part of our world, yet something we take for granted. Have you ever considered what your world would be like without sound? Your grandparents or great-grandparents may be able to relate to the time of silent movies or the time of listening to the radio before the days of television. Sound was the most important part of any radio program. A person could create a visual image of a radio show due to the dynamic sound effects. We still make use of those effects today.

Sound Effects Artist

Somewhere on a silent sound stage in Los Angeles, Shirley Wong is hard at work squishing jelly in front of a microphone. Far away on an Atlantic beach, Carlos Silva is crunching back and forth in a pair of clogs over spilled birdseed and recording the sound. Are they competing in some strange contest? No, Shirley and Carlos are sound effects artists.

You have heard the sounds they are recording when you listen to the eerie footsteps of outer space aliens coming toward you in movie theaters, or shivered at the slithery smooth sounds of monsters from the deep in a late-night movie.

Imagine being charged by a bull while recording a cow's moo for a milk commercial. Or how would you like to fall down the stairs on purpose just to tape the sound? Imagine trying out toys as part of your job, or shaking things in hardware stores, searching for just the right sounds. These are some of the situations you might find yourself in if you were a sound effects artist.

Before television became so commonplace, families sat around radios at night and listened to plays being read aloud. Thanks to the efforts of the sound effects artists, the radio audiences could hear the howls of an approaching tornado, the sounds of horses stomping at a hitching post, or the sound of a powerful foghorn in the English Channel. Working behind the voices of the characters, sound effects artists would pound coconuts into boxes of gravel to make hoofbeats or rattle pieces of tin to simulate storms or motorcycles coming down the street.

The job of a sound effects artist is not easy. It can sometimes take six people to make one sound. It requires strength, alertness, and perfect timing. Imagine a car crash on television with delayed crashing noises. If the sound of the impact came even one second late, it could ruin the effect. Good sound

Old radio broadcasts made use of sound effects.

effects bring listeners right into a story and make them feel like they are experiencing it with the characters.

Next time you take sounds for granted, turn off the sound on your television. In just a few minutes, you'll appreciate the work and creativity of sound effects artists like Shirley Wong and Carlos Silva.

Read With Sound Effects

Choose a chapter from one of your favorite books and develop sound effects to go along with it. Record these sounds and play them as you read the chapter aloud to your classmates, or have a friend help you demonstrate the sound effects as you read.

Sum It Up

In this lesson you studied the characteristics of sound. You found that some sounds are more familiar to your ears than others. You went on to discover that the way you hear sounds depends on certain properties of sound waves. Pitch is the highness or lowness of a sound as it is perceived. You found that as the frequency of sound waves goes up, the pitch rises and you hear a high sound. As the frequency of sound waves falls, the pitch drops and you hear a lower sound. Sounds are measured in units called hertz. The loudness of a sound is determined by the intensity of its sound waves. The intensity of the sound waves depends on the amount of energy that is put into the vibration from which the sound waves originate. The more intense the sound the more energy it carries as it moves along.

Using Vocabulary
loudness
pitch

Using no more than four characters, write a skit where two characters, Ms. **Pitch** and Mr. **Loudness,** demonstrate their characteristics (or personalities) as defined in this lesson. Humor might be one way you could develop the characters.

Critical Thinking

1. Suppose you had to determine which of two identical large sealed barrels was full of liquid, and which was only half full of liquid. How could you determine this if both were too heavy to move?
2. Describe how you could change the loudness of a sound produced by the plucking of a guitar string.
3. How could you change the pitch of a sound produced by a guitar string?
4. Compare and contrast pitch and loudness.
5. How does increasing the energy put into a sound wave affect its pitch and loudness?

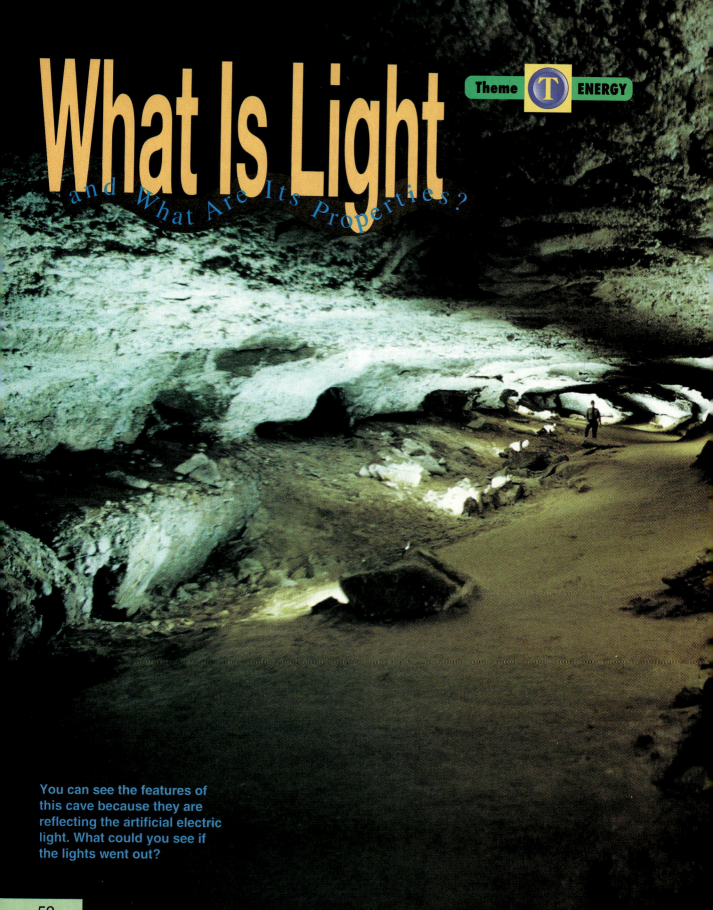

What Is Light and What Are Its Properties?

Theme T ENERGY

You can see the features of this cave because they are reflecting the artificial electric light. What could you see if the lights went out?

If there were no light, you wouldn't be able to see objects because they are only visible if they reflect light to your eyes.

Have you ever gone into a cave and explored its maze of tunnels? You can feel the damp coolness of the air inside. You can see the craggy rock walls in the beam of your flashlight. That flashlight is the key to your navigation. What if it falls and breaks? What if its beam flickers and fails? Up, down, forward, backward, everywhere you look total darkness surrounds you. You can't even see your hand in front of your face. How will you find your way out of the cave? Light is your link to safety and freedom.

TRY THIS Activity!

What Can You See in the Dark?

Try to hypothesize what you can see without light.

What You Need
dark room
***Activity Log* page 20**

Go into a windowless room or closet and close the door (first make sure you can open the door again from the inside). Turn off the light. What can you see? How long does it take your eyes to adjust? Can you see a glimmer of light from anywhere? Block the crack under the door with a towel so that no light creeps in around the edges. Now what can you see? How do you feel in complete darkness? Hypothesize how your life might be different without light. Record all answers in your ***Activity Log***.

Reflected sunlight is responsible for the moon's glow.

In the absence of all light, you see *nothing!* But it's hard to appreciate this because it's hard to find a place that is *totally* dark. It is easy to walk into a dark room and flick on an electric light. Because electric lights can be found almost everywhere, night is no longer an obstacle to doing most things. Even sports events such as football, baseball, tennis, and soccer are no longer limited to the daylight hours because many stadiums are equipped with electric lighting. But what if you lived a hundred years ago before electric lights were commonly used? A thousand years ago?

Ancient Egyptians made practical use of natural light. In many Egyptian houses, large windows called *clerestories* were cut into the upper living room walls that rose above the rest of the house. These windows allowed daylight to enter while maintaining the privacy of the family. Many contemporary homes make use of this ancient method of lighting.

Throughout history people in all cultures have found inventive solutions to lighting the dark. When Christopher Columbus and his crew came to the shores of North America in 1492, they saw palm tree torches being used by the Arawak (ar′ ə wak′) Indians. Thousands of kilometers across the ocean, Polynesians strung oil-rich nuts together and set them alight. Seven hundred years ago in China, Kublai Khan's (kü´blī kän´) soldiers burned lumps of fat fastened to the ends of sticks. The ancient Romans bound bundles of oil-soaked sticks together and set them ablaze at the tops of long poles. In the West Indies, hollow gourds were poked full of holes and filled with fireflies.

The Inuit, Native Americans who live in the Arctic, designed a lamp to provide light and heat inside their dwellings. The lamp was a piece of stone in the shape of a bowl. The wick consisted of dried grass. Fat from seals or walruses was used as fuel. When the wick was lighted, the heat melted the seal or walrus fat. The melted fat, now oil, soaked into the wick and burned.

Why is light vital for the very existence of our planet? Besides allowing us to see the world around us, the sun helps warm Earth. The light is used by green plants as they convert carbon dioxide and water into food in the process of photosynthesis. In this process, oxygen is released into the atmosphere. Without light, food, and oxygen, there would be no life on Earth.

Stored sunlight can be used to run cars, fly jets, grease motors, heat homes, pave roads, manufacture plastics, and generate electricity. As a matter of fact, most of the energy you use every day comes from sunlight, either directly or indirectly. Electrical energy can be generated from sunlight by solar cells. We use energy from the sun indirectly by burning coal that is formed from ancient plant material. Over thousands of years, the energy stored in these plants was changed into coal. When coal is burned, the energy stored in it is released. The same is true for oil and natural gas. These products come from the remains of organisms that obtained their energy from the plants they ate. So, what is light? What are the plants receiving from it? What warms us on a cold day and paints the sky with sunrises in the morning and sunsets at night?

Most objects we see do not emit light. Instead, when we look at these objects, we see the light from another source that bounces off the object. Moonlight is really sunlight that bounces off the moon toward Earth. It is because of this bouncing quality of light that we are able to see objects that do not emit their own light. Let's look at the next activity to observe this property of light.

EXPLORE Activity!

Reflection of Light

Light waves exhibit some of the same properties as sound and water waves. Remember that we learned about some of the properties of waves using a coiled spring? Recall what happened when the wave reached the end of the spring. The wave bounced back to you. Light waves can bounce in a similar manner.

What You Need

mirror
flashlight
transparent tape
string
protractor
Activity Log pages 21–22

What To Do

1 Place the mirror flat on the table as shown. Have one partner shine the flashlight at the mirror. Your partner needs to hold the flashlight steady in one position. From across the table, look at the mirror and move your head around until the brightness of the flashlight hits you in the eyes. You will notice that if you move out of that position, the bright light will no longer shine in your eyes.

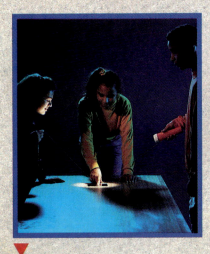 

2 Repeat the above procedure, but this time attach a string from the flashlight to the mirror. Use the tape for this. Have someone connect another piece of string to the mirror as you hold the other end in front of your eye when you are at the correct angle to see the bright light bouncing off the mirror.

3 Have that partner use the protractor to measure the angle that the string from the light makes with the mirror. Then have the same partner measure the angle that the string makes from the mirror to your eye.

4 Move the flashlight to different angles and measure the angle of light striking and bouncing off the mirror. Try angles of 15°, 30°, 45°, 60°, and 75°. Record all data in the chart provided in your **Activity Log**.

What Happened?

1. How did the beam of light from the flashlight in this activity seem to travel?
2. What is the relationship between the angles that you measured?

What Now?

1. What can you conclude about how light bounces off the surface of a mirror?
2. If the angle of the light striking the mirror is 0°, what would you predict the angle of the light bouncing off the mirror to be?
3. When you are looking at yourself in a mirror, what angle does the light that leaves your nose, strikes the mirror, and returns to your eye make with the mirror? Draw a sketch of this in your **Activity Log**.

EXPLORE

How Does Light Behave?

To understand how light can bounce off objects, you must first discover what light is. Light is a form of energy that is transmitted by waves. The energy in light is called **radiant energy.** Light waves are transverse waves like the waves you generated with the spring in Lesson 1. But unlike the sound and water waves you have studied so far, light waves can transmit energy in the absence of a medium. They can travel in a vacuum, a space that doesn't contain matter. Light, therefore, can move through the emptiness of outer space, through air, and many other substances.

Light waves are only one type of radiant energy. All radiant energy waves are called **electromagnetic waves.** Electromagnetic waves, like other kinds of waves, are caused by vibrations. These waves are produced by the vibrations of electric charges in atoms. The energy in electromagnetic waves is made up of electric and magnetic fields that vibrate at right angles to each other. You can demonstrate an electromagnetic wave with two ropes.

TRY THIS Activity!

Rope Waves

How can you demonstrate an electromagnetic wave?

What You Need
2 2m ropes
Activity Log page 23

Have a partner hold on tightly to the ends of two ropes of the same length. While you generate transverse waves moving vertically up and down in one rope, have a second partner generate waves of the same size moving side to side in the other rope so that the crests and troughs are in the same place. Draw a diagram in your **Activity Log** of the wave that was produced. In what direction does the energy move with respect to the wave?

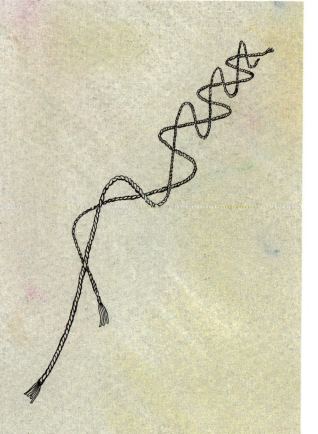

58

The wave you made with the two ropes models how electromagnetic waves move. The electric and magnetic portions of the wave pulse at right angles to one another as the wave moves energy forward in a straight line.

All electromagnetic waves are arranged in order by their wavelengths and frequencies on a chart called the **electromagnetic spectrum.** Light that you see is the only part of the electromagnetic spectrum that is visible to humans. Television signals, radio waves, ultraviolet radiation, X rays, microwaves, and infrared radiation are all forms of electromagnetic radiation.

All electromagnetic waves travel at the same speed: 300,000 kilometers per second (186,000 miles per second). They differ from one another only in frequency and wavelength. For example, gamma rays have shorter wavelengths and higher frequencies than radio waves. We see visible light because our eyes are sensitive to its particular frequency and wavelength.

The wavelength of visible light is so short that about 10,000 waves are needed to cover one centimeter of space. Storm waves on the ocean can have wavelengths of up to 180 meters (600 feet) or more; some of the longer radio waves can have wavelengths of up to 10,000 meters (32,800 feet). We will focus our study of electromagnetic waves on visible light, but keep in mind that all forms of electromagnetic radiation exhibit similar properties.

Literature Link

Nutty Knows All

Choose a friend who has read *Nutty Knows All* by Dean Hughes. Pretend that you are Nutty and your friend is William Bilks. Write a character sketch about Nutty, including the things he does and why. Your friend should write a character sketch about William. The two of you should concentrate on characteristics of the two that would allow each of them to try and attempt a science fair project where light waves can communicate with the brain. Compare Nutty's and William's ideas about the properties of light waves to those you have learned in this lesson. Could Nutty's experience have actually happened? Why or why not? If you were to present a science fair project on light waves, what would you present? What previous knowledge about light waves would be helpful to know? Record all information in your *Activity Log* on page 24.

Radio telescopes receive electromagnetic waves.

Electromagnetic Spectrum

Visible light: The wavelength of visible light is 10^{-6} m. The different wavelengths of visible light appear as the colors of the rainbow. These wavelengths combine and make up white light.

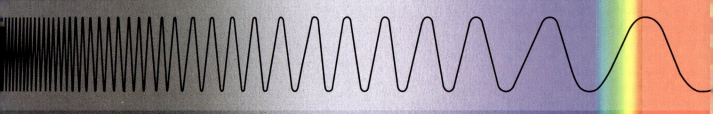

Gamma rays: The wavelength of a gamma ray, 10^{-15} m, is shorter than an electron. Gamma rays can penetrate human tissue.

UV rays: Ultraviolet rays, 10^{-7} to 10^{-4} m, are present in sunlight. The sun's UV radiation is what makes the pigments in our skin change when we tan or burn. Sunscreen lotion can block these rays.

X rays: The wavelength of an X ray, 10^{-9} m, is about the same as the width of one atom. X rays can penetrate the body's soft tissue. Photographs of the shadows of X rays can show the bones inside your body.

Infrared radiation: Infrared wavelengths, 10^{-6} to 10^{-3} m, are given off by warm objects. Special infrared cameras can see the heat given off by warm objects as infrared light.

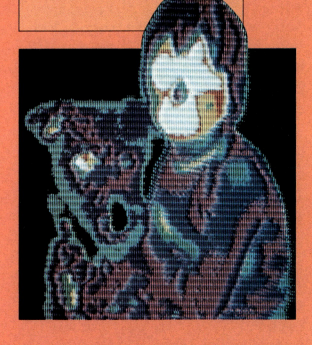

Microwaves: The wavelength of a microwave is 10^{-3} to 1 m. Microwaves used for cooking vibrate the molecules in food very rapidly. Friction between the molecules generates heat and cooks the food.

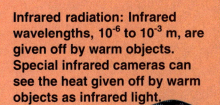

Radio waves: The wavelength of a radio wave is 10^{-1} to 10^{5} m. Radios and televisions work on the energy of invisible radio waves.

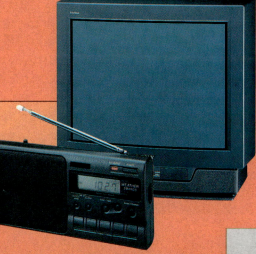

Light: Yesterday and Today

Humankind has tried to explain the properties of light ever since our species has existed. Early humans observed the sources of light such as the sun and stars, or a campfire. Some early cultures, such as the Greeks, Romans, and some Native Americans, made up myths and legends to explain the mysteries of light. It was thought long ago by early Greeks that light went *from* the eye to the object being seen. If something blocked the path of that light, the object vanished from sight. The idea that we see things because of the light that is reflected from them to the eye was first suggested by an Arab mathematician, Alhazen, in about A.D. 1000 in a published work called *Optics*. Alhazen attempted to explain why things farther away appeared smaller in size. His theories about light and reflection were much more advanced than other theories of his time.

Think back to the Explore Activity in which you shined the light from a flashlight to a mirror so that the light reflected off the surface of the mirror at different angles. You discovered that changing the angle of light hitting the mirror also changed the angle of light that was reflected off the mirror's surface. Light, as well as all other electromagnetic waves, has the ability to bounce off some surfaces. The angle at which the electromagnetic waves are reflected depends on the angle of the waves striking the surface and the shape of that surface.

You can model the way light waves reflect with a basketball. Imagine you're in the last minute of a basketball game. Your team is down one point and a teammate is positioned perfectly to make a basket. You have the ball! It's time for a bounce pass. You toss the ball onto the floor, and it bounces once directly into your teammate's hands. She shoots and makes a basket. The ball hits the floor and bounces upward with equal angles. Knowing the principle of reflection helped your team win the game.

In the activity with the mirror and the flashlight, you investigated the same principle. By changing the angle of light from your flashlight to the mirror, you changed the angle of light from the mirror to your line of vision. The changes in the angles were equal every time.

A mirror reflects light to form an image. Mirrors are usually made of a sheet of glass with an aluminum or silver coating on the back. Almost any smooth surface can act as a mirror. Have you seen boats tied to a dock on a still day? They seem to be moored on a mirror. If a breeze blows up, ripples scatter the glassy reflection on the water. You can observe the differences in reflection on smooth and rough surfaces in the Try This Activity on the next page.

The smooth glassy surface of this lake reflects images almost as well as a plane mirror.

TRY THIS Activity!

Comparing Light Reflection

You can compare how light reflects off a smooth and a rough surface.

What You Need
aluminum foil, flashlight, *Activity Log* page 25

Lay a smooth piece of aluminum foil on a flat surface such as a table. Shine the light from the flashlight on the foil and observe the reflection. Now, crumple the foil into a ball. Shine the flashlight onto the ball and observe the reflection. Smooth out the foil onto a flat surface again, shine the light on it, and observe the reflection. How does the reflection of light from the crumpled foil differ from the reflection from the smooth piece? Hypothesize what would happen to light that is reflected from any rough surface. Record all observations and hypotheses in your *Activity Log*.

Light can continue to be reflected from one mirror to another.

Other Properties of Light

When light rays reflect from a glossy or shiny surface that is smooth, almost all the rays reflect in the same direction. However, most objects do not have this quality. When you shone the light onto crumpled aluminum foil, you found that when light reflects from a surface that is not glossy or shiny *and* smooth, the rays reflect in different directions. The crumpled foil is shiny but not smooth. Therefore, light striking a surface like this is scattered and no image is produced. That is why you can see your reflection on the smooth surface of a pond until a light breeze causes ripples to form and break up the image.

What you see when you stand in front of a mirror is actually an image of yourself. Light falling on you reflects off of you onto the mirror. Some of that light is reflected from the mirror back to your eyes.

Minds On! Imagine you are looking into a mirror. Draw a diagram in your *Activity Log* on page 26 that represents the path that light travels between your face and the mirror. Now, imagine again that you are looking at your face in the mirror. Describe the image you see in your *Activity Log*. Be sure to note the size of your image, how far behind the surface of the mirror it appears to be, and whether it is right side up or upside down. Next, touch your right ear with your right hand. Imagine how your reflection appears as you do this. Which hand appears to touch which ear in the image formed in the mirror?●

The reflection you imagined in the last activity should have appeared to be the same size you are and right side up, but reversed. When you imagined touching your right ear with your right hand, you should have "seen" the opposite, touching left hand to left ear. You also probably pictured your reflection in the mirror to be the same distance behind the mirror as you were in front of it. Of course, nothing is really behind the mirror; it only appeared that way. To observe another property of light, try doing the activity below.

Whenever you look into a mirror, the image you see appears to be turned around.

TRY THIS Activity!

Traveling Light Rays

You can observe how white light travels from its source.

What You Need
chalk dust, penlight flashlight, *Activity Log* **page 27**

Clap two chalkboard erasers together, then shine a penlight flashlight through the dust cloud. How did the light travel? Why can you see the path of the light so well in the dust cloud? Record these answers in your *Activity Log*.

When you shone the flashlight into the chalk dust, you found that light waves travel in a straight line from their source, like spokes radiating out in all directions from the hub of a wheel. We sometimes refer to light that moves out from a source as light *rays* because they are much easier to diagram as straight lines. When a ray of light reaches an object, several things can happen. As you have already observed, it can be reflected and bounce off the object at an angle equal to its incoming angle. Sometimes light rays can pass through an object and bend slightly from their original path. Light rays can also be absorbed by an object. What frequently happens is a combination of these things. You will observe more about how light is bent and absorbed by objects in the next two lessons. However, performing the next Try This Activity can help you understand how light can reflect from and pass through an object.

64

TRY THIS Activity!

What Happened to the Light?
You can observe how light can reflect from and pass through an object.

What You Need
notebook paper, mayonnaise, light source, *Activity Log* **page 28**

Have you ever been doing your homework and eating a sandwich at the same time? Just as you're about to finish writing one page, a blob of mayonnaise falls out of your sandwich and onto the page. Rub a little mayonnaise into a sheet of notebook paper. Do you see a dark spot right in the middle of the paper? Now hold the paper up in front of a light source. How does the spot appear now? You may observe that it is brighter than the rest of the page. Why does the spot appear dark when the paper is on the table and bright when you hold it up in front of a light? Record all observations in your ***Activity Log***.

The oil in the mayonnaise penetrated the fibers of the paper and filled in the spaces between them. The oil made that spot smooth and uniform compared to the rest of the paper, so light passed through the spot more easily. Remember that light travels in straight lines. When your notebook paper was on the desk, light passed through, or was absorbed by, the spot but reflected off the rest of the paper toward your eyes. When you held your paper up to a light, most of the paper looked darker because most of the lamp light was reflected away from you on the other side. The spot looked brighter because you saw the light passing through it like a stained glass window.

The flower, like the paper that was unstained by mayonnaise, is opaque. Opaque (ō̄ pāk′) **materials do not allow any light to pass through them.**

Objects that allow light to pass through them without forming a clear image are called translucent (trans lü′ sənt). **The vase, like the greasy blob on the paper, is translucent.**

Objects that allow light to pass through them and enable you to see images clearly are transparent. What are other examples of transparent, translucent, and opaque objects?

65

Applications of Light

Light, with its many properties, can be used in a variety of ways to make life both interesting and easier for us. One such application of light is in the use of a periscope (per′ ə skōp). A periscope is an optical instrument with which a person can view objects from a distance. Periscopes are used in submarines and other weapons to observe objects above the surface of the water. Scientists and engineers make use of the periscope to observe objects without endangering themselves. Try the next activity in which you can make a periscope to see around corners.

TRY THIS Activity!

Make a Periscope

A shiny, smooth surface like a mirror reflects light rays to form an image. You can make a periscope to observe how plane mirrors can reflect light so that you can see around corners.

What You Need

2 small plane mirrors, ballpoint pen, triangular piece of cardboard, scissors, tall empty milk carton, Activity Log page 29

1. Using the triangular piece of cardboard, draw two diagonal lines on one side of the carton and cut a slot along each of the lines as shown.
2. Draw two similar lines on the other side of the carton, directly opposite the slots you have already cut. Cut slots along those lines also.
3. Insert the plane mirrors into the slots so that their reflecting surfaces face one another.

4. Draw a large square directly in front of the top mirror and cut it out with the scissors.

5. Make a small hole in the back of the carton with the pen. Be sure that the hole is level with the bottom mirror.
6. You have made a periscope. Now use your periscope to see around barriers.
7. Draw a diagram of your periscope in your *Activity Log* and show how the light rays travel through the periscope and into your eye. Predict what would happen if you changed the angle of one or both mirrors.

Have you ever watched a late-night war movie in which the commander of a submarine ordered, "Up periscope!" The periscope on a submarine is a lot like the one you made with the mirrors. You used your periscope to see around corners; similarly, a submarine commander uses the periscope to see above the surface of the water. Both periscopes work in the same manner—they reflect light so an image can be viewed from an angle.

If the plane mirror is curved inward like the inside of the bowl of a spoon, it becomes a concave mirror. A concave mirror doesn't reflect light in the same way as a plane mirror does. It converges light rays from a distant source. If a light source is placed directly in front of a concave mirror, the light rays reflect outward in a parallel pattern. You see this effect every time you observe the beam of light from a flashlight, spotlight, or car headlight. If a plane mirror is curved outward, like the outside of the bowl of a spoon, it is called a convex mirror. A convex mirror diverges light rays outward. Convex mirrors are often called wide-angled mirrors because they produce images with greater fields of vision than plane and concave mirrors. For this reason, these mirrors are often used when a wide-angle view is desired. Convex mirrors are used as security mirrors in stores and as side-view mirrors in cars and trucks.

A light bulb placed directly in front of a concave mirror can reflect parallel light rays.

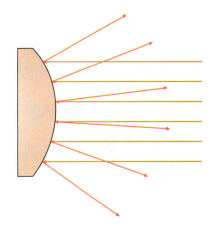

Parallel light rays striking a convex mirror reflect outward as shown.

A convex mirror is thicker in its middle than on its edges.

Minds On! Have you ever stood in front of the fun house mirrors at a carnival? These mirrors make you look tall and skinny, short and fat, or weird and wavy. Can you hypothesize what is happening to the angle of reflected light in these mirrors? In your *Activity Log* page 30 illustrate what you think is happening to the light rays as they reflect from these mirrors.

Fun house mirrors reflect light in a variety of ways, often causing an image to be distorted.

When you look into a fun house mirror, you can see how irregular curves can cause a distorted image to be formed. Similarly, irregular curves in any plane mirror can cause an image to be distorted.

 Focus on Technology

The Hubble Telescope

In 1990 a large orbiting mirror telescope, named after the astronomer, Edwin Hubble, was launched into Earth's orbit. The purpose of launching this telescope into space was to increase its light-gathering abilities so that, with it, we can obtain clearer images of objects in space. As a result, we hope to gain a better understanding of the universe.

After the telescope was placed in orbit, it began sending images to Earth. These images were somewhat blurry. The problem was with an irregular curvature in the telescope's 240-centimeter mirror. It distorted the image produced just like a fun house mirror.

In 1993 astronauts from the space shuttle Endeavour repaired the telescope. A camera with built-in mirrors was installed to correct the blurry image. The result is a near perfect picture sent back to Earth.

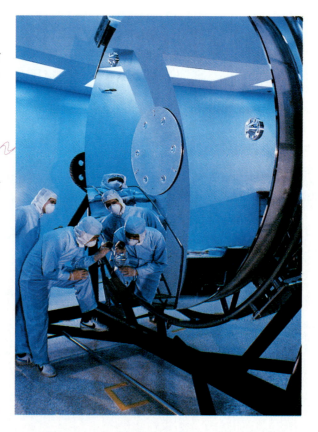
Bypassing Earth's atmosphere allows the Hubble Telescope to obtain clearer images of objects in space.

Sum It Up

In this lesson you learned that the electromagnetic spectrum includes gamma rays, X rays, ultraviolet rays, radar signals, microwaves, and radio and television signals. You saw how these waves of radiant energy travel at the same speed, varying from one another only in wavelength and frequency. Throughout this lesson it has been evident that electromagnetic waves can transmit energy in the absence of a medium. Light is the only part of the electromagnetic spectrum that humans can see. Investigation of light waves demonstrated that light waves travel in straight lines from their source and that they can be reflected from a shiny object. You observed how images are produced in plane mirrors. You found that when light reflects from a rough object, the rays are scattered. You also observed how light rays pass through transparent, translucent, and opaque materials.

Using Vocabulary

electromagnetic spectrum
electromagnetic waves
opaque
radiant energy
translucent
transparent

Using the vocabulary words introduced in this lesson, write a description or action of specific objects in your home, school, or other environment. Your description or action should be explained in a manner that clearly reflects the definition of each word being used.

Critical Thinking

1. Describe the arrangement of electromagnetic waves on the electromagnetic spectrum.
2. How are light waves reflected from a plane mirror?
3. Describe how electromagnetic waves travel through space.
4. Differentiate between plane mirrors and concave and convex mirrors.
5. Describe why it is not possible to see objects when there is no light.

Refraction—
What Happens When Light Is Bent?

The refraction of light creates an optical illusion of the moon.

Can you always believe what you see when an object is reflected back to you? In this lesson you'll observe a very interesting property of light—refraction.

Imagine crossing the Sahara desert on foot. You've walked for miles and miles, hours and hours. The last drop of water has been drained from your canteen. Even your camel couldn't take it. You stagger, ready to give up, when all of a sudden a shimmering lake appears before your eyes. You lick your parched lips and lurch forward, ready to plunge into a vast sea of...sand. Light has played a trick on you. The shimmering lake is not there. It is only a mirage (mi räzh′).

Hopefully you have never been in such circumstances. However, it is possible that on a hot day, you have seen a puddle of water on the highway in front of you, only to have it disappear when you come to that stretch of the road. What causes these mirages? How can light create false images? You have studied light. You know that light transmits energy through waves. In the previous lesson, you investigated how light travels in straight lines from its source; and you also read that light can transfer energy even in the absence of a medium. In this lesson, you will explore another important property of light. You'll find out how light can be bent. To help you visualize this property, do the Try This Activity.

TRY THIS Activity!

Is This Real?
What property of light makes an object appear to be bent when it is viewed in a different medium?

What You Need
writing pencil, tall plastic jar, tap water, *Activity Log* page 31

Put the pencil in the tall plastic jar of water such that about half of it is submerged. Observe the pencil from several angles. What does the water do to the light passing from the pencil to your eyes? Record your observations in your *Activity Log*.

Have you ever stood at the edge of a swimming pool and talked to someone standing in waist-deep water? The swimmer, like the pencil in the glass of water, looks funny and out of proportion. The swimmer's legs appear to be much too short in proportion to the body that is above the water line. This is because light is bent at the surface of the pool as it passes from the water into the air. The same thing happens to the light coming from the pencil that you see in the water. What are other examples of light being bent as it moves between two mediums?

EXPLORE Activity!

How Can You Bend Light?

In the Try This Activity on page 71, you saw how light can sometimes be bent. In this exploration, you will try to find out how the angle of the light affects how it is bent.

What You Need

large sheet of butcher paper
clear rectangular pan
centimeter ruler
pen
water
small opaque container
coin
Activity Log pages 32–33

What To Do

1. Trace the outline of the pan on the piece of paper as shown in the photograph. Remove the pan and draw the lines 1, 2, 3, and 4 on the paper with a ruler as shown.

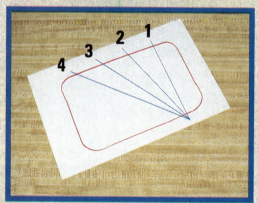

2 Put the pan back on its outline on the paper and fill the pan with water to a depth of 5 cm.

3 Look through the side of the pan (through the water) along line number 1. Hold your pencil behind the pan on the opposite side and try to line the pencil point up with line number 1. Mark the point on the paper where the pencil and line number one appear to meet.

4 Repeat this process with lines 2, 3, and 4.

5 Remove the pan of water and measure how far away from the lines your pencil marks are. Record your observations and results in your *Activity Log*.

What Happened?

1. How close to the lines were your four pencil marks? Did you notice any pattern?
2. Why do you think you missed the lines with your pencil?

What Now?

1. Why were you able to correctly put your pencil on line number 1?
2. Why was there greater error in your mark for line number 4 than in your mark for line number 2?
3. Work with a partner. Sit up in a straight position at a table. Put a coin in the center of a small opaque bowl. Hold still while your partner gradually moves the bowl away from you in a straight line. Tell your partner to "Stop!" at the exact moment the coin is no longer visible over the edge of the bowl. Have your partner slowly fill the bowl with water without moving the coin. What happens? Can you see the coin? How can you use what you learned in the water pan activity to explain this "reappearing" coin trick?
4. Answer all questions and record all observations in your *Activity Log*.

What Is Refraction?

On television game shows, people race one another to win prizes. They sometimes do strange things in the process. Imagine being a contestant on such a show. You have to swim through a pool, race across a room, burst through a wax paper wall, and dive into a tub of gelatin. Chances are you are not moving in a straight line as you encounter these obstacles. You turn and twist and bounce in all different directions as you race from water to air to solid to something in between. Light rays may also bend as they move through different mediums.

Another name for light rays being bent is **refraction** (ri frak′ shən). With your pencil lines and the pan of water, you learned that light is not bent, or refracted, when it passes through water at a right angle. As its angle to the water increases, the bending of the light rays increases.

Just as game show contestants can't always race forward in a straight line, so also can light be bent as it travels through different mediums.

Think of light as a game show contestant. Light waves travel constantly through different mediums. In air, light travels in straight lines and at constant speeds in all directions. When light waves encounter another medium, they may speed up or slow down, depending on the nature of the medium. This happens because different mediums have different densities. The molecules of one medium may be packed together more tightly or loosely than those of its neighboring medium. Light passing into a more dense medium slows down. Likewise, light passing into a less dense medium speeds up.

Glass, for example, is more dense than air. When sunlight strikes a window, it travels across the boundary from air into glass and it slows down. That's because it can't move as quickly through the tightly packed molecules of the glass. The speed of light in air is 300,000 km per second (186,000 miles per second). In glass its speed slows to 197,000 km per second (118,200 miles per second). If you know this, you can also predict that when light passes from one medium to another at an angle, it will change in speed and direction.

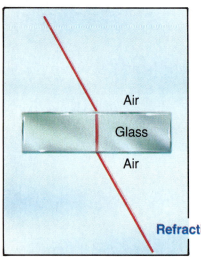

Refraction of light rays

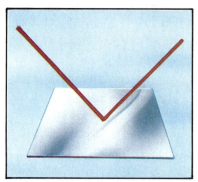

Reflection of light rays

Refraction and You

Imagine you are racing down a sidewalk on roller skates. The wheels of one skate veer off the sidewalk onto the grass. The skate in the grass slows down. The skate on the sidewalk is still going fast. What happens to you? You turn away from your original path down the sidewalk and shift toward the slower skate. Suddenly you're moving over the grass at a considerably slower speed. This is similar to the way light changed speed and direction as it passed from the air to the water in the Explore Activity that you did on pages 72 and 73.

If you went roller skating down a straight sidewalk toward grass at the bottom of a hill, both of your skates would hit the grass at the same time. They would slow down together by the same amount, so neither skate could pull you to one side. You would keep going in a straight line. You have slowed down, but not changed direction.

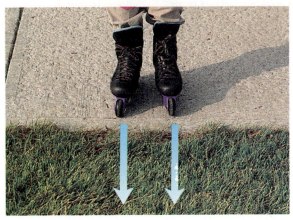

Like the skates in the above photograph, when the light struck the water at a right angle, it slowed but didn't refract.

Remember the "trick" using light that was discussed at the beginning of this lesson? The shimmering lake on the desert, or the pool of water appearing on the highway in front of your car on a hot summer day are nothing more than mirages, a word that comes from the Latin word, *mirare* (mir ä′ re), meaning "to look at." Mirages are caused by hot air near the surface of Earth. Look at the illustration to the right.

Because warm air is less dense than cool air, its molecules are more loosely packed. As a result, light can travel with greater speed through warm air. When light rays move from cool air to hot air, they are refracted along our line of vision. The light rays are bent from the sky toward our eyes. What looks like water on the pavement or in the sand, is really a refracted image of the sky.

Mirages can even occur in the sky. When hot layers of air hover near the surface of the ocean, people at sea sometimes see images of distant ships upside down in the sky. Do you think some strange sightings reported as "flying saucers" may actually have been images similar to mirages?

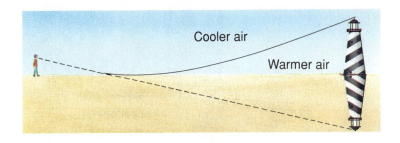

Is It Concave or Convex?

You saw in the last lesson that mirrors produce images by reflecting light in straight lines. Lenses, however, produce images by refracting light as it passes through them. A **lens** is a transparent object that has at least one curved side. Most lenses are made of transparent glass or plastic that has been carefully ground and shaped. Some are even made of quartz crystals. Lenses are used to magnify or reduce images, or to concentrate or separate light rays.

One of the most common uses for lenses is to correct vision. If you wear eyeglasses or contact lenses, you know that lenses can help you see better by making blurry images appear clear. If you've ever watched birds perched at the tops of trees or football players scattered across a stadium, you know that the lenses in binoculars can make distant objects seem closer and bigger. Tiny cells become visible under the lenses of a microscope. Faraway objects take on a definite shape when viewed through a telescope. A family gathering may be recorded through the eye of a camera lens. Can you think of other uses for lenses? In order to understand the properties of lenses, try the next activity.

Activity!

Observing Lenses

How can you observe how some lenses bend light rays?

What You Need

several types of convex and concave lenses,
flashlight, small plastic comb, small amount of clay, *Activity Log* page 34

Use the clay to stand the comb on end, as shown. Place the flashlight about 10 cm in front of and pointed at the comb. Turn the flashlight on.

Observe the shadows formed by the teeth of the comb and sketch what you observe in your *Activity Log*. Place the lens between the comb and the flashlight. Move the lens back and forth, observe, and write what you observe about the shadows again. Do you observe any differences? Sketch these results in your *Activity Log*. Repeat this same procedure for each type of lens. From your observations, what's your conclusion as to how lenses affect light rays?

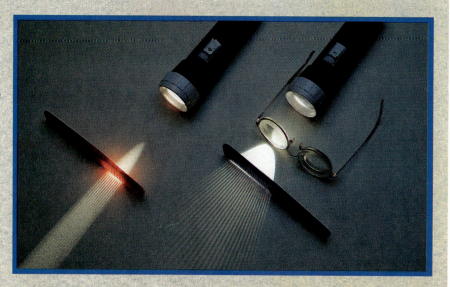

Despite their many and varied uses in our lives, there are really only two basic kinds of lenses—concave and convex. Light bends when it passes through either kind. Lenses that are thicker in the middle than at the edges are called **convex lenses.** Parallel rays of light traveling into a convex lens are bent toward one another so they meet, or converge, at a point on the other side. The point where these light rays converge is called the **focal point.** The distance from the focal point to the lens is the focal length. A detective's magnifying lens is convex. Microscopes are made up of two convex lenses.

parallel rays of light

rays converge

focal point

convex lens

Convex lenses are also used to correct a vision problem called farsightedness. People who are farsighted have a lens in the cornea of the eye that does not focus light on the retina. Because the focal length is too long and the focal point is located behind the retina, these people see blurry images when looking at objects nearby. Wearing glasses with convex lenses will cause light rays to begin to converge before they enter the lens in the eye. As a result, the images formed by the light will focus correctly on the retina, and the resulting vision will no longer be blurry.

Lenses that are thicker at the edges than at the center are called **concave lenses.** Light rays passing through a concave lens diverge, or spread away from one another. Concave lenses are used in cameras and to correct nearsightedness. Nearsighted people's eyes focus images of distant objects in front of the retina. Their focal length is too short, and they have trouble seeing distant objects clearly. Concave lenses correct this by diverging the light entering the eye so that it extends the focal length and causes light to focus properly on the retina.

Have you ever turned on a slide projector and found the image on the screen to be fuzzy? But when you adjust the lens, the image comes into sharp focus. Concave lenses do the same thing for nearsighted eyes.

A light ray passing directly through the center of a concave or convex lens keeps its original direction. Rays striking the lens anywhere else but the exact center are bent. The amount of bending, or refraction, increases with distance from the center of the lens, and the amount of curvature in the lens affects the focal length.

parallel rays of light

rays diverge

concave lens

Minds On! Think of and list the various kinds of lenses you experience in your daily life. Classify them as either concave or convex. How do each of these lenses affect the light that passes through them? In your *Activity Log* page 35, draw an illustration showing how a combination of convex and concave lenses will refract light.●

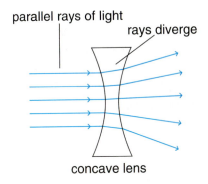

Does this water drop form a concave or convex lens?

77

Uses of Lenses

What do microscopes, contact lenses, cameras, and your eyes have in common? They all contain curved, transparent structures called lenses. Lenses have increased our knowledge and understanding of the world and the universe surrounding us. Understanding how lenses make images of objects is important so we can learn more about the objects we view through them.

Lenses at Work

How can you investigate some properties of a convex lens?

What You Need

strong magnifying lens, flashlight, scissors, electrical tape, plain sheet of white paper, meter tape, Activity Log page 36

1. Hold the magnifying lens above a piece of white paper.
2. Shine a flashlight through the magnifying lens from above.
3. Move the magnifying lens up and down so the light rays passing through the convex lens converge to form a circle of light. You will see the circle of light grow smaller and brighter, then bigger and less distinct as you move the lens up and down over the paper.
4. See if you can find the exact point at which the circle of light on the paper is smallest and brightest. Any motion up or down will diminish its intensity. When you find this point, you have found the focal point of your magnifying lens. This is the point at which all of the refracted light rays converge as they pass through the lens.
5. Cut an arrow shape out of electrical tape. Place it on the center of the magnifying lens, and hold the lens between the flashlight and the paper. What happens to the arrow as you move it slowly up and down above the paper? What happens to the arrow at the same distance from the paper as the focal point you found in step 4?
6. Now hold the magnifying lens at arm's length and study your classroom through the lens. Look out the window. Look at your friends. Are the images you see right-side up or inverted?
7. While looking through the magnifying lens, slowly and steadily zoom in close on something small and distinct.
8. If the image you see is inverted, look for the exact moment when the inverted image you see turns right-side up. Measure the distance between the magnifying lens and the object when this occurs. Repeat this observation several times with different objects. When you have found the exact point at which this switch takes place, you have again found the focal point of the magnifying lens.
9. In your **Activity Log,** draw a scale drawing to represent step 8. Be sure to label the focal point and focal length.

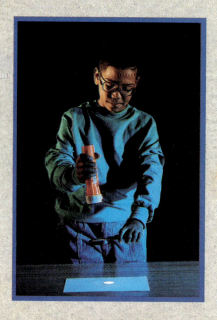

A drop of water can be a lens that acts like a magnifying glass. What do you perceive in this photograph?

Language Arts Link

Words and Lenses

Lenses change the way we perceive objects and events. Words can also change our perceptions of objects and events. When you read a poem or story, your mind forms images based on the words you read. In your *Activity Log* on page 37, write about the ways in which language and lenses are similar and different. Give several examples of this phenomenon.

Light waves bring the world to your brain through your eyes. But the eyes do not actually "see" at all. The cornea and lens of your eye work like convex lenses to focus light rays on the retina, the innermost wall of the eye. The retina acts like a switchboard operator. Light-sensitive cells in the retina change the energy of the light to electric signals that are then sent to the brain. The brain interprets the signals as the upright images we think we are "seeing."

Why must images be focused on the retina in order for us to see? The retina is thin and extremely fragile tissue. It's made up of cells called rods and cones, named for the shapes they have. The center of the retina houses 6,000,000 cones that are sensitive to colors and bright lights. It's the cones that produce sharp images of objects and scenes on which the eyes are directly focused. The outer edges of the retina house 120,000,000 rods. The rods aid in night vision because they are more sensitive to dim light than are the cones. Have you ever noticed that when the lights are suddenly turned off it takes a few minutes for your eyes to adjust to the dark? When this happens, all those rods are working to help you perceive images in very dim light. Rods don't respond to colors—that's why it's very difficult to detect colors in the dark.

Pigment, or colored material, in the rods and cones absorbs even the smallest particles of light striking the retina. The pigment in the rods, called visual purple, lets the eyes see shades of gray and also lets them see in dim light. Though you can see images in reduced light, you can't perceive color. Three different pigments in the cones absorb blue light, green light, and red light. They enable the eyes to see colors and sharp images in bright light. These three pigments together allow us to distinguish more than 200 different colors!

Nerve fibers attached to the rods and cones join at the back of the retina to form the optic nerve. The optic nerve consists of about a million fibers that act like a flexible cable connecting the eyeball to the brain. The optic nerve carries the electric signals produced by the retina in response to light waves. The brain interprets those signals as visual images and color.

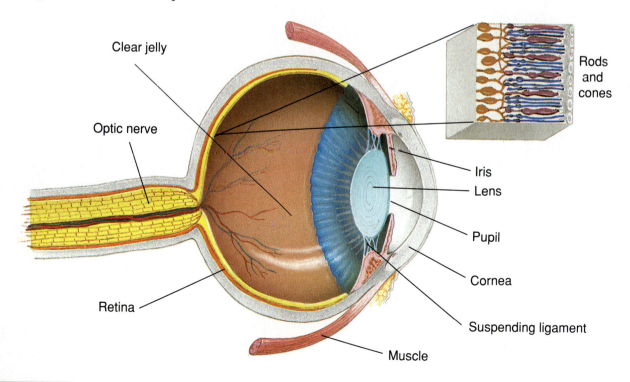

Sum It Up

In this lesson you discovered that electromagnetic waves, including light rays, can be bent. The bending of light as it passes from one medium to another is called refraction. As light crosses the boundary between media of different density, it changes speed and direction. Lenses use this principle of refraction to produce images. Without lenses we would not be able to see. Your eyes contain lenses. Concave and convex lenses adjust focal lengths, and enlarge or reduce images to improve our vision of the world. Light-sensitive cells, called rods and cones, make up the retina of the eye. These cells absorb light and convert it to electric signals that are relayed to the brain. Pigments in the cones allow us to distinguish colors.

Using Vocabulary

concave lenses
convex lenses
focal point
lens
refraction

Write a definition for each of the vocabulary words introduced in this lesson. Then use each word in a sentence that reflects your understanding of the word in a real-world application.

Critical Thinking

1. Why do olives appear larger when they are inside a curved glass jar?
2. Draw a concave and a convex lens and show how each bends light rays.
3. What is the purpose of a convex lens in a camera?
4. How are mirages related to refraction?
5. What would happen to light rays that pass through both a convex lens and a concave lens?

Theme T ENERGY

How Does a Prism Separate White Light Into Colors?

Have you ever seen a rainbow in the midst of water sprinkling from a garden hose? In this lesson, you will observe many examples of white light being separated into colors.

Colors play an important role in protecting this tiger beetle from its predators.

What do rainbows, tiger beetles, prisms, and comic strips have in common? They all display brilliant colors and optical illusions. Tiger beetles have evolved protective camouflage to hide from predators. If they live in thick vegetation, such as lush forest, they are bright green. In this environment they can sit on green leaves and be undetected. Likewise, as desert-dwelling beetles run across a dry creek bed, they appear to be dull brown and mottled gray, the colors of the stones and sand around them. The tiger beetle's brown color is perfect camouflage in the desert sand. It vanishes from sight and survives another day. The wings of these beetles have evolved to match the colors of their habitats. When they blend into the scenery around them, the tiger beetles appear almost invisible to the birds and lizards that might eat them.

Have you noticed the beautiful colors on a compact disk (CD)?

Since the beginning of time, people have marveled at the brilliant colors of a rainbow.

A prism is a piece of cut glass that displays all colors of the visible spectrum.

If you captured a desert tiger beetle and examined it under a microscope, you would see that its front wings are covered with tiny metallic spots of blue-green color coming from reflecting pits that are surrounded by red. When you first picked up the beetle, it appeared to be brown. A predator, too, sees a brown beetle. How can these tiny spots of blue-green and red appear brown from a distance? Why don't these beetles appear to be spotted with blue-green and red?

The same thing happens when you look at a color comic strip in a magazine or the Sunday newspaper. If you look at the colors from a distance, they appear to be solid. However, if you look at them very closely, you will probably see a series of tiny dots in different colors. This technique of creating colors using tiny dots is quite common. Some artists even use these dots to blend colors in their paintings. As a matter of fact, the colors you see on your television screen are actually made up of thousands of tiny dots of red, green, and blue. You can explore this effect in the following activities.

TRY THIS Activity!

Color Images

How can you create images using only small points of three basic colors?

What You Need

red, blue, and yellow pencils or pens
Activity Log page 38

Select a small object and draw it in your **Activity Log** using only small dots of the colors red, blue, and yellow placed closely together. Will the drawing look the same from a distance as it does up close? Predict the colors you will see from a distance and write your prediction in your **Activity Log**. Step back and look at your completed drawing from a distance. Do you still see dots of color, or have your colors appeared to have merged and changed the effect of your drawing? Hypothesize why this happens.

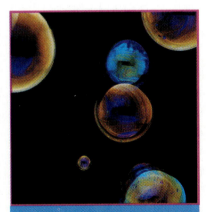

Bubbles—enlarged circles of water—display the same colors as rainbows and prisms.

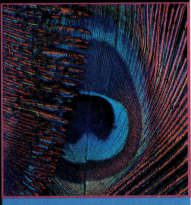

Use a magnifying glass to look at this photograph. What do you see?

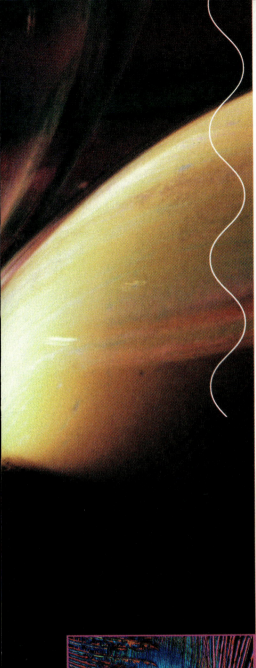

EXPLORE Activity!

Spinning Color

How can you develop a model that shows you ways to explore how colors interact with each other?

What You Need

stiff paper
scissors
centimeter ruler
paper clip
coloring pens
pencil
Activity Log pages 39–40

What To Do

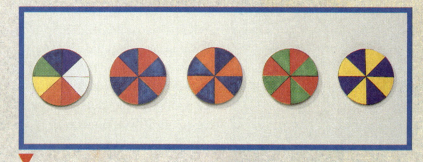

1 Cut out five round color wheels, about 13 cm in diameter, from stiff paper. Divide the wheels into 8 equal parts with a ruler and pencil.

2 Color each section on one wheel with different colors of the spectrum, leaving two-eighths of the wheel white. Use the colors red, orange, yellow, blue, green, and violet for the colored segments.

3 Make four wheels with only two colors each. On each wheel, color every other section of the wheel with the colors listed below:
 Wheel #1 red & blue
 Wheel #2 orange & blue
 Wheel #3 red & green
 Wheel #4 violet & yellow

4 Straighten the paper clip, leaving the hook at the top. Poke the long tail of the paper clip into the center of a wheel and spin it. Leave the hook above the wheel to keep it from flying away as you spin it.

5 Predict what will happen to the colors when you spin each of the wheels, and write your predictions in your *Activity Log*.

6 Spin each of the wheels in turn. Record your observations in your *Activity Log*.

What Happened?

1. What colors did you see in the full color wheel that had all colors and white?
2. What colors did you observe in each of the other wheels? How did your predictions compare with your observations?
3. What do your results tell you about ways colors are used in nature?

What Now?

1. Look very closely at a black and white newspaper photograph. What do you see?
2. Examine a color photograph in a magazine. How do you think the image of the photograph you see is related to the color wheels you made?
3. Can you think of other examples of separated or merged colors that you may encounter every day?

EXPLORE

Formation of Colors

Recall from the previous lesson that you are able to see most objects because of light that is reflected from another source. These objects produce no light of their own. You have just observed in the color wheel activity and by drawing a picture with dots that the colors of objects also affect how we see them. You may wonder what makes objects appear to be certain colors. To learn the answer, you first have to understand what it is that we refer to as white light. White light is a mixture of all colors of the visible spectrum. White light must be present in order for us to see any colors. You see colors of various objects because they reflect light. Do the Try This Activity with the prism on this page to find out more about white light.

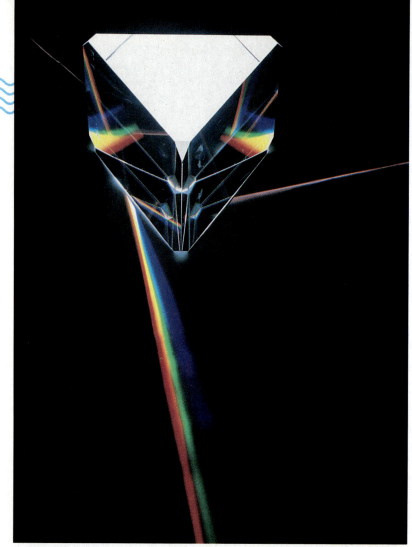

A **prism** (priz′ əm) is a triangular piece of glass or plastic.

TRY THIS Activity!

White Light and Colors: What Makes Up White Light?

How can you use a prism to observe the colors that make up white light?

What You Need

prism, sunlight, paper (to be used as a screen), colored pencils, *Activity Log* page 41

Place the prism between a window and the paper. Allow a ray of sunlight to pass through the prism and to the paper. How does the prism change the white light? You should notice a spectrum of colors projected on the paper. Write down the colors you see in your *Activity Log*. If two prisms are available, see what happens when a second prism is placed between the first prism and the screen. Predict the color of light that will result. Use colored pencils to illustrate the effect in your *Activity Log*.

When you passed white light through the prism, you saw all colors of the spectrum. That happened because white light is actually made up of all those colors. The colors of the spectrum are red, orange, yellow, green, blue, indigo, and violet. When white light is passed through a prism, these colors separate according to their wavelengths. Each wavelength of light always refracts by a different amount as it travels through a prism. This results in the familiar pattern of colors seen in spectra produced by refracted light.

Colors with shorter wavelengths are refracted more than those with longer wavelengths. For this reason, violet light (with the shortest wavelength) is refracted the most. Red light (with the longest wavelength) is refracted the least.

You know that starlight appears white. But did you know that different stars emit spectra of different wavelengths? Williamina Fleming, an astronomer born in Dundee, Scotland in 1857, did extensive study on star spectra. Her study on the spectral emission of stars led to the discovery of hundreds of stars and 10 novae.

Think about a rainbow you may have seen in the sky after a storm. Have you ever tried to follow its arc with your eyes, looking for that mythical pot of gold? A ray of sunlight enters a raindrop and gets refracted, breaking it into the colors of the spectrum. When the refracted ray strikes the inner surface of the raindrop, it is reflected and turned back in the opposite direction. When the refracted-reflected ray travels out of the raindrop and into the air, it is refracted once again. The beautiful rainbow you see is the result of the refraction and reflection of white light in millions of water droplets.

The seven colors of a rainbow are the same as the ones you saw refracted in the prism.

Each raindrop forms many colors, but the color that reaches our eyes from a particular raindrop depends on the angle between it and the line formed by the sun's rays. Many raindrops, each sending colored light at certain angles, form a complete rainbow.

You see a rainbow when the sun is behind you and the sky in front of you is filled with moisture. The drops of water in the sky act like tiny prisms.

Can Colors Be Deceiving?

Did you know that the light reflected from the moon can cause rainbows to occur? The less intense lunar light produces colors that are more faint than those of sunlight, but otherwise they are just the same as daytime rainbows. Think about other places that you may have seen rainbows.

Many optical illusions are caused by the reflection and refraction of light. Recall the discussion of mirages in the previous lesson. Here, refracted light creates a false image of something that isn't where it appears to be. Similarly, rainbows and colored light are also formed by reflection and refraction. Colored lights can also affect the way we see objects.

Keep this idea in mind as you read the next few paragraphs.

Have you ever been shopping for new clothes, and noticed in the dressing room that your skin color looked odd—possibly washed out? Maybe you even tried something on, bought it, and noticed that the color seemed different the first time you wore it. What caused the color of your skin and the color of the clothes you bought to appear different in and out of the store? Perhaps there were mostly bright fluorescent lights in the store that made everything appear slightly blue or green. Outside in the sun, things usually appear more yellow. Why is this so?

You could hypothesize that the light inside the store was somehow different from the sunlight. Next, you might think

Observe how different colored lights affect the color of this dalmation.

Light reflected from the moon can result in a display of less intense colors than those produced by the sun.

about different situations that involved a variety of lighting effects. For example, maybe you were at a picnic last summer. As the sun began to set and dusk approached, you may have noticed the colors of the things around you fading in the dim light. If there was an ultraviolet bug light nearby, you may have noticed your white shirt beginning to glow in the dark!

Likewise, if you've ever been sitting in a theater when the lighting technicians were trying different colors of lighting on the stage, you may have noticed that the curtains appeared to change color with each color of light being shone on them. Maybe you've stood under a blinking sign at night and seen how peculiar people look in the colors cast by the neon light. Clothes, hair, teeth, skin...look totally different. You can probably think of many more unusual lighting situations you have observed. How did the color of the light affect the appearance of the objects? Think about how colors change in dark and daylight.

When you describe the color of an object, you are usually describing it in sunlight or lamplight, both of which are called white light. You know that a ripe banana looks yellow in white light. How will it look in red light or blue light? Try the Try This Activity and see.

The color you see when you look at an object depends on the color of light it reflects. An object that looks red in white light appears that way because it absorbs all the colors of the spectrum *except* red. The red light is reflected off its surface.

Think about what happened in the activity with the colored lights. If you used a red light, and it caused an object to appear nearly black, it absorbed almost all the light and reflected very little back. If this object was green—say, a plant—it appears black in red light because it absorbs all light with the wavelength of the red. In white light the plant also absorbs the red light and reflects only the green light. Therefore, it appears to be green. What color would you expect the plant to appear in green light?

Is This a Color Test?

How can you test if the colors of objects will appear different under different lights?

What You Need
rubber band
flashlight
cellophane (red, green, blue)
Activity Log page 42

Shine a flashlight on several objects of different colors. Write down the name of the object and its color in your **Activity Log**. Cover the flashlight with red, green, and blue cellophane. Before you turn it on, predict the color that each object will appear when you change the color of the cellophane. Write your prediction in your **Activity Log**. Now, turn on the flashlight. Were your predictions correct? What colors did the objects actually appear to be? Record your observations In your **Activity Log**. What is your prediction as to how these objects would appear in another color of light? If possible, test this prediction. Test as many different colors as you can. Record all observations in your **Activity Log**.

Using a prism, you've discovered that white light is a mixture of all the colors of the spectrum. You also discovered how each color has its own wavelength and refracts differently from the other colors.

Have you ever seen weird lights that look like colored hair standing on end, waving around eerily under a glass dome? Those lamps are made with fiber optics. To understand this better, try the next activity.

Pouring Light

You'll observe how light is affected by a stream of water.

What You Need
tall, slim transparent jar with lid
masking tape
water
flashlight
oak tag (firm, dark poster paper)
pan or pail
Activity Log page 43

1. Fill the jar about 2/3 full of water. Put the lid on. Then cover the holes with masking tape so the water doesn't spill out.
2. Roll the oak tag around the jar, covering it completely. It should look like a long paper log. When you have done this there should be extra paper extending past the bottom end of the jar.
3. Put the flashlight inside the paper roll. The beam end of the flashlight should touch the bottom of the jar.
4. Turn on the flashlight. Hold the oak tag tube so the jar is upright. Take the tape off the lid.
5. Darken the room. Using the large nail hole as a spout, turn the jar and flashlight assembly on its side and pour the water into the pan.

From your observations, answer the following questions in your *Activity Log*.

How can you pour light with water? What makes it stay within the boundaries of the water medium? If you repeated the activity with colored cellophane between the flashlight and the jar, do you think you would be able to pour colored light? Would color make any difference in the results?

Technology of Light

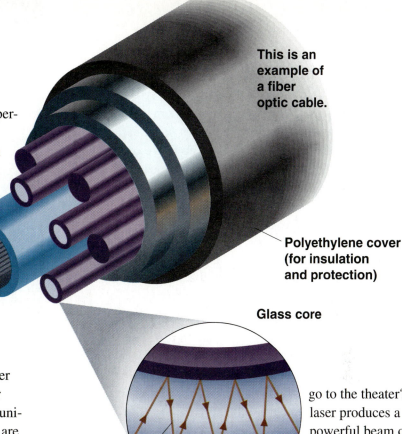

This is an example of a fiber optic cable.

Polyethylene cover (for insulation and protection)

Glass core

Light signals

Core

You modeled how fiber optics work when you performed the Try This Activity on page 92 in which you poured light with water. The water acted like a fiber optic cable. The light stayed inside the water because of total internal reflection. But there are many other practical uses for fiber optics. Do you know anyone who has ever had exploratory surgery? Fiber optics make that easier. Fiber optics are also used in communication. Many telephone calls are transmitted using light as a signal via fiber optics. Fiber optics were first discovered in England in 1955. Fiber optics are sometimes called light pipes. The fibers used are often thin strands of glass. Regardless of how the fiber is bent, light flows along on the inside of the fiber. The light is totally internally reflected within the fiber.

The light conducted along the inside of a fiber is usually laser light. When you think about lasers, the first thing you think of may be a movie you have seen in which the characters fight off rebel invaders with laser guns in outer space. Have you ever played laser tag? *Laser* actually stands for *Light Amplification* by *Stimulated Emission* of *Radiation*. Can you remember all that next time you

There are many practical uses for fiber optics.

go to the theater? A laser produces a very powerful beam of light that has enough energy to cut a hole through steel. Unlike white light, laser light contains only one color of the spectrum. Recall that each color of light has its own wavelength and frequency. Likewise, a particular color of laser light has the same wavelength and frequency. The crests and troughs of these waves stack up in a way similar to the way lasagna noodles stack up in a box.

This light is so uniform that it is called "coherent" light. White light, on the other hand, is called "incoherent" because white light radiates from its source in all

93

directions and at different wavelengths and frequencies.

For this reason, astronomers use lasers for measuring instruments because laser beams move in a straight line and don't spread out like the light from a flashlight. The *Apollo* astronauts, who landed on the moon in 1969, left behind a mirror to reflect laser light. A laser beam fired from Earth to hit the reflector will bounce back to Earth. The time it takes for the laser beam to travel to the moon and back is measured. Using this information with the speed of the laser—the same as for all electromagnetic waves—astronomers can determine the distance between Earth and the moon that is accurate to within 15 centimeters!

Literature Link

Optics: Light for a New Age

Another use of lasers with which you are probably most familiar is that used for reading Universal Product Codes (UPCs). Whenever you buy groceries, school supplies, books, or clothing, the cashier might scan the product label across a plastic window or scan it with a small laser gun. When the product is scanned, you can observe a thin red beam of light. That is the laser. It is used to "read" the UPC code.

Collect the UPCs from labels of products you have at home. Study the UPCs and classify them into groups based on their characteristics. Can you figure out what the black bars mean?

To help you research UPC codes on products, refer to the book *Optics: Light for a New Age* by Jeff Hecht.

Although lasers are becoming more and more common all the time, you may be more familiar with other forms of light. In your home, at school, or in the shopping mall you read about earlier, you rely on fluorescent and incandescent bulbs to see clearly. Fluorescent lights are tubular electric lamps containing mercury vapor and coated on the inside with a phosphor. Light hitting the phosphors, which are fluorescent substances, is absorbed, stored for a short period, and then emitted. Some fluorescent lamps emit visible light that closely approximates daylight, but many produce light that is mostly in the blue-green part of the spectrum. This accounts for

Fluorescent lights are used in advertising

Tube

Mercury vapor
Phosphor coating
Cathode
Lead-in wires

Fluorescent tube

94

the unusual hue some colors have in fluorescent light.

Bright fluorescent lights are found everywhere today—in classrooms, businesses, and homes. Scientists are now discovering that this type of illumination may not be good for everyone.

Fluorescent lights may be more harmful to people than dimmer incandescent light bulbs because the intensity of the light can be overstimulating. Too much light can make it difficult for students to sit still, especially after spending six to eight hours a day under fluorescent lights. The over-stimulation of a too-bright environment can make it harder to sleep at night. Sleeping patterns are thrown off for some people because they are no longer tied to the natural cycle of day and night.

Have you ever gone camping or stayed on an island without electricity? After a period of adjustment, you probably learned to live with softer, more natural illumination. Studies have shown that people who function in an environment that has incandescent lighting are not as tired, stressed, or irritable at the end of the day as those who work in fluorescent lighting. Incandescent light seems to have a calming effect on many people. Which type of light do you prefer to use?

Sum It Up

In this lesson, you observed how white light can be refracted into the colors of the spectrum. You can communicate how rainbows form in the sky. Raindrops act like tiny prisms and separate white light into spectral colors. Each color has its own specific wavelength and angle of refraction. Most objects appear to have color because certain wavelengths are reflected and others are absorbed. You discovered that the color objects appear to be depends largely on the color of light they reflect. You also observed that colored light makes objects appear to be different colors than white light. Unlike white light, laser light contains only one color. The waves of laser light move together at the same wavelengths and the same frequencies. We need light to see but some types of light can be overstimulating and stressful to some people's eyes.

Using Vocabulary

prism

Refresh yourself with the definition of *prism*. Focusing on the definition, illustrate the concept of a prism with a small art project that would take you no more than 30 minutes to complete.

Critical Thinking

1. Describe how you can separate the colors of white light. What are the colors?
2. What determines an object's color?
3. How would you expect a red object to appear in green light? Why?
4. How many times is light refracted as it passes through a prism?
5. How could you refract the colors of the spectrum back together to form white light?

Waves in Your World

Throughout this unit you've learned that you're completely surrounded by waves every minute of every day. You have studied the common properties of water waves, sound waves, light waves, and the rest of the electromagnetic spectrum. You've investigated, as well, some of the properties that distinguish each kind.

Waves are energy carriers. Water waves can bob a toy boat or destroy an island. Seismic waves move through Earth, changing the face of continents. Sound waves keep us in touch with the world. Light waves allow us to see the world, live on it, and thrive.

TRY THIS Activity! How Will You Communicate With the World?

Using the information you have learned about waves, develop a communication system. Imagine your classroom is an information broadcasting station. Develop a communication code, using sound, light, water, mirrors...anything you can think of. Write a broadcast schedule using the 24-hour clock used by all shortwave stations and ships at sea. How will you communicate with the world and what will you tell them? Include all information in your *Activity Log* page 44.

Minds On! A hurricane is sweeping into an isolated fishing village on the coast. Imagine you are in charge of rescue operations. Danger alerts, food and shelter, medical assistance, entertainment, and weather tracking...are under your command. Think of all the ways you can put waves to work for you. Don't forget there are many different kinds of waves—water, sound, light, microwaves, X rays, radio waves, television signals. List all the wave applications you can think of in your *Activity Log* page 45.

Imagination is the only limitation in utilizing wave energy.

GLOSSARY

Use the pronunciation key below to help you decode, or read, the pronunciations.

Pronunciation Key

a	at, bad		d	dear, soda, bad
ā	ape, pain, day, break		f	five, defend, leaf, off, cough, elephant
ä	father, car, heart		g	game, ago, fog, egg
âr	care, pair, bear, their, where		h	hat, ahead
e	end, pet, said, heaven, friend		hw	white, whether, which
ē	equal, me, feet, team, piece, key		j	joke, enjoy, gem, page, edge
i	it, big, English, hymn		k	kite, bakery, seek, tack, cat
ī	ice, fine, lie, my		l	lid, sailor, feel, ball, allow
îr	ear, deer, here, pierce		m	man, family, dream
o	odd, hot, watch		n	not, final, pan, knife
ō	old, oat, toe, low		ng	long, singer, pink
ô	coffee, all, taught, law, fought		p	pail, repair, soap, happy
ôr	order, fork, horse, story, pour		r	ride, parent, wear, more, marry
oi	oil, toy		s	sit, aside, pets, cent, pass
ou	out, now		sh	shoe, washer, fish mission, nation
u	up, mud, love, double		t	tag, pretend, fat, button, dressed
ū	use, mule, cue, feud, few		th	thin, panther, both
ü	rule, true, food		<u>th</u>	this, mother, smooth
u̇	put, wood, should		v	very, favor, wave
ûr	burn, hurry, term, bird, word, courage		w	wet, weather, reward
ə	about, taken, pencil, lemon, circus		y	yes, onion
b	bat, above, job		z	zoo, lazy, jazz, rose, dogs, houses
ch	chin, such, match		zh	vision, treasure, seizure

amplitude (am′ pli tüd′) the greatest distance the particles in a wave rise or fall from their rest position

cochlea (käk′ lē ə) a spiral tube inside the inner ear that changes the sound waves into electrical signals and sends them to the brain

concave lens a lens thinner in the middle than at the edges; refracts light rays away from each other

convex lens a lens thicker in the middle than at the edges; refracts light rays toward each other

crest (krest) the high point of a wave

decibel (des′ ə bəl) the unit to measure the volume or loudness of sound

echo ranging a method of measuring distance, which may be helpful in locating objects or distances to those objects we can't see

electromagnetic spectrum (i lek′ trō mag net′ ik) transverse energy waves, ranging from low frequency to very high frequency, that travel at the speed of light in a vacuum; includes radio, infrared, visible, ultraviolet, x rays, and gamma rays

electromagnetic wave (i lek′ trō mag net′ ik) a wave in which the energy is made up of electric and magnetic fields that vibrate at right angles to each other

focal point the place that all light rays from a parabolic mirror or convex lens pass through

frequency (frē′ kwən sē) the number of waves that pass a point in a given unit of time

hertz (hûrts) the unit of wave frequency equivalent to one cycle per second

lens a curved, transparent object; usually made of glass or clear plastic

light energy the only visible part of the electromagnetic spectrum

longitudinal wave (lonʹ ji tü´ də nəl) A wave in which matter vibrates in the same direction as the wave moves

loudness describes a person's response to sound intensity; loud sounds produce a sound wave with a large amplitude

mirage (mi räzhʹ) an optical illusion caused by the bending of light rays by layers of air having different densities and temperatures

opaque (ō pākʹ) material that does not allow light to pass through it

optic nerve a nerve that consists of about a million fibers that acts like a flexible cable connecting the eyeball to the brain

periscope (perʹ ə skōp) an optical instrument with which a person can view objects around corners

pigment a colored material that absorbs certain colors of light and reflects other colors

pitch the way a person hears the frequency of a sound; in general, the greater the frequency, the higher the pitch

prism (prizʹ əm) a triangular piece of glass or plastic with two straight faces at an angle to each other; refracts light twice; produces visible light spectrum

radiant energy energy that can travel through space in the form of waves

refraction (ri frakʹ shən) bending of a wave or light ray, caused by a decrease in speed as it passes from one material into another at an angle

rogue wave a wave that is produced by water waves that are "in phase." Rogue waves have been known to reach 30 meters

translucent (trans lüʹ sənt) material that transmits light, but does not allow you to see clearly through it

transparent having the property of transmitting or passing light

transverse wave (trans vûrsʹ) a wave in which matter vibrates at right angles to the direction in which the wave travels

trough (trôf) the valley of a wave

vibration (vī brāʹ shən) rapid back and forth movement

wavelength the distance between a point on one wave to the same identical point on the next wave

INDEX

Alhazen, 62
Amplitude, 19; *illus.,* 19; of sound, 46
Archytas, 42
Aristotle, 42

Berger, M., 11
Book reviews, 10, 11
Branley, Franklin M., 11

Carter, Alden R., 11
Camouflage, 83; *illus.,* 83
Careers, fishing with sonar, 36–37; sound effects artist, 50–51
Cochlea, of ear, 49
Cochlear implants, 49; *illus.,* 49
Coherent light, 93
Colors, 82–97; *act.,* 85, 86–87, 88, 91, 92; changing of, 90–92; formation of, 88–89; wavelengths of, 89
Compression, *illus.,* 32
Concave lenses, 77
Concave mirror, 67; *illus.,* 67
Cones, of eye, 80
Convex lenses, 77; *act.,* 78
Convex mirror, 67; *illus.,* 67
Cornea, 80
Crest, 18, 22; *illus.,* 18, 32

Decibels (dB), 46–47

Earthquake-safe building, 23–25
Earthquake waves, 8, 23–25
Echolocation, 37
Echo ranging, 36
Electromagnetic spectrum, 59
Electromagnetic Spectrum, The, (Branley), 11
Electromagnetic waves, 8, 58–59; *act.,* 58; speed of, 59, 94
Energy, radiant, 58
Energy transfer, 7, 8, 13, 20, 21; *act.,* 17; *illus.,* 6, 12, 13
Environment, and noise pollution, 34–35
Exploring With Lasers, (Filson), 11
Eye, 80; lens of, 77, 80

Farsightedness, 77
Fiber optics, 93; *illus.,* 93
Filson, Brent, 11
Fluorescent light, 94–95; *illus.,* 94
Focal point, 77
Frequency, 18; measuring, 44–45; of sound waves, 42–45; *act.,* 43

Galileo, 43
Gamma rays, 59; *illus.,* 60

Health, noise and hearing loss, 48–49
Hearing, threshold of, 47
Hearing aids, 49
Hearing loss, 48–49
Hecht, Jeff, 10, 94
Hertz, Heinrich, *illus.,* 44
Hertz (Hz), 44
Hubble, Edwin, 68
Hubble telescope, 68; *illus.,* 68
Hughes, Dean, 11, 59
Hurricane, 97; *illus.,* 97

Incoherent light, 93
Interference, 22–23; *act.,* 22
Iris, 80

Laser, 93–94
Lens, 76–80; *act.,* 76; concave, 77; convex, 77; *act.,* 78; of eye, 77, 80; uses of, 78
Light, 52–69; *act.,* 53; *illus.,* 54; applications of, 66–68; *act.,* 66; coherent, 93; fluorescent, 94–95; *illus.,* 94; incoherent, 93; properties of, 62–65; *act.,* 63, 64, 65; reflection of, 62–65, 89, 90; *act.,* 56–57, 63, 65; *illus.,* 62, 63, 64, 67, 74; refraction of, 70–81, 89, 90, *act.,* 72–73, 76, 78; *illus.,* 74, 75; technology of, 93–95; traveling of, 64–65; white, 82, 88–89, 91, 92; *act.,* 88, 92

100

Lights, Lenses, and Lasers (Berger), 11
Light rays, 64–65; focal point of, 77
Light waves, 7, 58–59; *illus.,* 8; speed of, 20, 59, 74, 94; wavelength of, 59, 89; *illus.,* 61
Longitudinal waves, 32; *act.,* 32; *illus.,* 32
Loudness, 45–49; *act.,* 45

Marconi, Gugielmo, 43
Matter, 8
Microwaves, *illus.,* 61
Mirage, 75
Mirror, 67–68; *illus.,* 62, 63, 64; concave, 67; *illus.,* 67; convex, 67; *illus.,* 67; fun house, 68; *illus.,* 68; plane, 67; *act.,* 66

Nearsightedness, 77
Noise pollution, 34–35
Nutty Knows All **(Hughes)** 11, 59

Ocean waves, 8–9, 38, 39
Opaque materials, 65
Optical illusions, 83, 90
Optic nerve, 80
Optics: Light for a New Age **(Hecht),** 10, 94

Periscope, 66–67; *act.,* 66
Pitch, 42–43; *act.,* 43
Plane mirrors, 67; *act.,* 66
Pollution, noise, 34–35
Prism, 82–85, 88–89, 92; *act.,* 88; *illus.,* 84, 88
Pupil, 80
Pythagoras, 42

Radiant energy, 58
Radio: From Marconi to the Space Age **(Carter),** 11

Radio waves, 59
Rainbow, 89, 90; *illus.,* 84, 89
Rarefaction, *illus.,* 32
Reflection, 62–65, 89, 90; *act.,* 56–57, 63, 65; *illus.,* 62, 63, 64, 67, 74
Refraction, 70–81, 89, 90; *act.,* 72–73, 76, 78; *illus.,* 74, 75
Retina, 77, 80
Rods, of eye, 80
Rogue wave, 22

Seismic waves, 8
Smart building, 23–25
Sonar, 36–37
Sound, 26–51; amplitude of, 46; communicating with, 30; *illus.,* 35; loudness of, 45–49; *act.,* 45; noise pollution, 34–36; producing, 31; *act.,* 28–29, 31, 40–41; *illus.,* 30, 31; properties of, 42–43; *act.,* 43; speed of, 33, 34
Sound effects artist, 50–51
Sound frequency, measuring, 44–45; pitch and, 42–43; *act.,* 43
Sound waves, 7, 8; *act.,* 32; *illus.,* 9; action of, 32–33; frequency of 42–45; intensity of, 46–47; *illus.,* 47
Spectrum, electromagnetic, 59

Tank waves, *act.,* 19
Telescope, 68; *illus.,* 68
Threshold of hearing, 47
Townshend, Pete, *illus.,* 48
Translucent materials, 65
Transparent materials, 65
Transverse wave, 17; *illus.,* 16, 32
Trough, 18; *illus.,* 18, 32

Ultraviolet rays, *illus.,* 60
Universal Product Codes (UPCs), 94

Vibrations, 30; *illus.,* 31
Visual purple, 80

Water waves, 8, 17; *illus.,* 8, 9, 13, 39
Wave crest, 18, 22; *illus.,* 18, 32
Wave interference, 22–23; *act.,* 22
Wavelength, 18; *illus.,* 18, 32; of colors, 89; of light waves, 59, 89; *illus.,* 61
Wave machine, *act.,* 21
Wave motion, *act.,* 9, 21; factors affecting, 20
Wave properties, 12–25; *act.,* 14–15, 19; *illus.,* 18–19; amplitude, 19, 46; frequency, 18, 42–45; length, 18, 59, 89
Waves, 7–9; electromagnetic, 8, 58–59, 94; *act.,* 58; energy transfer by, 7, 8, 13, 20, 21; *act.,* 17; *illus.,* 6, 12, 13; light, 7, 20, 58–59, 74, 89, 94; *illus.,* 8; longitudinal, 32; *act.,* 32; *illus.,* 32; rogue, 22; seismic, 8; sound, 7, 8, 32–33, 42–43, 46–47; *act.,* 32; *illus.,* 9, 47; transverse, 17; *illus.,* 16; water, 8, 17; *illus.,* 8, 9, 13, 39
Wave speed, 20; electromagnetic, 59, 94; of light, 20, 59, 74, 94; of sound, 33, 34
Wave tank, *act.,* 19
Wave trough, 18; *illus.,* 18, 32
White light, 82, 88–89, 91, 92; *act.,* 88, 92

X rays, *illus.,* 61

CREDITS

Photo Credits:

Cover, The Image Bank/ Michael Tcherevkoff; **1,** Uniphoto; **3** (t) ©Studiohio, (b) J. Zimmerman/FPG International; **6, 7,** ©Comstock Inc.; **8,** (l) Darrell Jones/The Stock Market, (r) Craig Aurness/Westlight; **9,** (t) NASA, (m) ©Russ Kinne/Comstock Inc., (bl) J. Zimmerman/FPG International, (br) Jon Feingersh/The Stock Market; **10, 11,** ©Studiohio; **12, 13,** ©Studiohio/location courtesy of Sawmill Athletic Club; **13,** (b) Superstock; **14,15,** ©Platinum Studios; **16,** Uniphoto; **17,** ©Studiohio; **18, 19,** Robin Smith/Tony Stone Worldwide/Chicago Ltd.; **21,** ©Studiohio; **23,** ©Wesley Boexe/Photo Researchers; **26,** (l) Janet Gill/Tony Stone Worldwide/Chicago Ltd., (m) T. Tracy/FPG International, (r) ©Stewart Cohen/Comstock Inc.; **26, 27,** Bill Ross/Westlight; **27,** (l) Paul Steel/The Stock Market, (m) John Terence Turner/FPG International, (r) ©Tony Angermayer/Photo Researchers; **28,** ©George Anderson; **29,** ©Studiohio; **30,** ©Dr. Gary Settles/Photo Researchers; **31,** The Bettman Archive; **34,** ©Kent Wood/Photo Researchers Inc., (inset) J. W. Packard/The Stock Market; **34, 35,** Ted Horowitz/The Stock Market; **38,** (l) George B. Gibbons III/FPG International, (m) FPG International, (r) ©Russ Kinne/ Comstock Inc.; **38, 39,** Mike Moir; **39,** (l) Kent Knudson/FPG International, (m) Stan Osolinski/The Stock Market, (r) J. Scowen/FPG International; **40, 41,** ©Studiohio; **42,** (l) ©Topham/The Image Works, (r) Guy Marché/FPG International; **43,** (l) ©Topham/The Image Works, (r) ©Platinum Studios; **44,** ©Keystone/The Image Works; **44, 45,** ©KS Studios; **45,** ©Studiohio; **47,** Chisholm Rich/The Stock Market; **48,** ©1982, John Roca, LGI; **50,** ©NBC Photo/FPG International; **52, 53,** ©Russ Kinne/Comstock Inc.; **54, 55,** ©Harald Sund; **56, 57,** ©KS Studios/1991; **59,** Tony Stone Worldwide/Chicago Ltd; **60,** (tr) Randy Taylor/Gamma Liaison, (ml) The Telegraph Colour Library/FPG International, (b) Chris Bjormberg/Photo Researchers; **61,** (tr) ©K.S. Studios/1991, (ml) Dr. R. P. Clark & M. Goff/Photo Researchers, (br) Courtesy of Sony Electronics; **62,** Tony Stone Worldwide/Chicago Ltd.; **63,** ©Richard Megna, Fundamental/Photo Researchers; **64,** (t) ©Platinum Studios, (b) ©Brent Turner/BLT Productions/1991; **65,** ©Brent Turner/BLT Productions/1991; **66,** ©KS Studios/1992; **67,** ©Henley & Savage/The Stock Market; **68,** (t) Bill Ross/Westlight; (b) NASA; **70, 71,** NASA; **72, 73,** ©Platinum Studios; **74,** ©MTV Networks; **75,** ©Doug Martin; **76,** ©George C. Anderson; **77,** ©Platinum Studios; **78,** ©KS Studios; **79,** ©Steve Terrill; **82, 83,** E.R. Degginger; **83,** ©Mark Mattock/Planet Earth Pictures; **84,** (l) ©Comstock Inc., (m) ©Lew Eatherton/Photo Researchers, (r) David Sutherland/Tony Stone Worldwide/Chicago Ltd.; **84, 85,** Brownie Harris/The Stock Market; **85,** (l) Thaine Manske/The Stock Market, (r) David Wagner/The Stock Market; **86, 87,** ©Studiohio; **88,** Pete Saloutos/The Stock Market; **89,** Charles Krebs/The Stock Market; **90,** (l) ©Jeff & Glenn Durham, (r) ©KS Studios; **93,** Michael Keller/FPG International; **94,** Ross Rappaport/FPG International; **96,** (t) David Seawell/Westlight, (b) ©Lawrence Migdale/Photo Researchers.

Illustration Credits:

16, 18, 19, 36, 61, 74, 75, 92, 94, James Shough; **24,** David Reed; **33, 89,** Thomas Kennedy; **46, 93,** Ann Larson; **49, 80,** Harriet Phillips; **58,** Veronica Mack; **60,** Hima Pamoedjo